Edward de Bono is the leading authority in the field of creative thinking and the direct teaching of thinking as a skill. While there are thousands of people writing software for computers, Edward de Bono is the pioneer in writing software for the human brain. From an understanding of how the human brain works as a self-organising information system, he derived the formal creative tools of lateral thinking. He is also the originator of 'parallel thinking' and the Six Thinking Hats. His tools for perceptual thinking (CoRT and DATT) are widely used in both schools and business.

Edward de Bono's instruction in thinking has been sought by many of the leading corporations in the world such as IBM, Microsoft, Prudential, BT (UK), NTT (Japan), Nokia (Finland) and Siemens (Germany). The Australian national cricket team also sought his help and became the most successful cricket team in history.

A group of academics in South Africa included Dr de Bono as one of the 250 people who had most influenced humanity in the whole course of history. A leading Austrian business journal chose him as one of the twenty visionaries alive today. The leading consultancy company, Accenture, chose him as one of the fifty most influential business thinkers today.

Edward de Bono's methods are simple but powerful. The use of just one method produced 21,000 ideas for a steel company in one afternoon. He has taught thinking to Nobel prize winners and Down's syndrome youngsters.

Edward de Bono holds an MD (Malta), MA (Oxford), DPhil (Oxford), PhD (Cambridge) and DDes (RMIT). He has had faculty appointments at the universities of Oxford, Cambridge, London and Harvard and was a Rhodes Scholar at Oxford. He has written 67 books with translations into 37 languages.

how to have

A BEAUTIFUL MIND

EDWARD DE BONO

LONDON

3 5 7 9 10 8 6 4

First published in the United Kingdom in 2004 by
Vermilion, an imprint of Ebury Press
Random House UK Ltd
Random House
20 Vauxhall Bridge Road
London SW1V 2SA

Random House Australia (Pty) Limited
20 Alfred Street, Milsons Point, Sydney
New South Wales 2061, Australia

Random House New Zealand Limited
18 Poland Road, Glenfield
Auckland 10, New Zealand

Random House (Pty) Limited
Endulini, 5A Jubilee Road, Parktown 2193, South Africa

Random House UK Limited Reg. No. 954009
www.randomhouse.co.uk
Papers used by Vermilion are natural, recyclable products
made from wood grown in sustainable forests.

A CIP catalogue record is available for this book from the
British Library.

ISBN: 0091894603

Printed and bound in Great Britain by
Mackays of Chatham plc, Chatham, Kent

✿ contents

✦ introduction

WHAT IS A BEAUTIFUL MIND?

There is this beautiful woman at a cocktail party. She has flawless skin, elegant clothes and a perfect figure. Surprisingly, she seems to be much on her own. People come up to her and quickly drift away.

Then there is this short, balding and mousy man. He is always surrounded by people in animated conversation with him.

What is going on?

You can do a great deal to make your body more beautiful. There are exercises at the gym. There are nips and tucks and liposuction and inserts.

You can do much to make your face more beautiful with cosmetics and even plastic surgery. A man can have hair implants.

But what about your mind? Do you make any effort at all to have a beautiful mind? Great physical beauty with a boring mind is boring. You might get attention but you will never keep that attention.

At the cocktail party the beautiful woman had a boring mind and the mousy man had a beautiful mind. That is why the man got more attention than the woman.

So what can you do to make your mind more beautiful?

You are born with a certain shape of face and body. There is only a certain amount you can do to make them more beautiful. But there is very much more that you can do to make your mind more beautiful. That is exactly what this book is about. This book tells you what to do to make your mind more beautiful.

If you have natural physical beauty it is a tragedy to waste this beauty by having a boring mind. It is like buying an expensive car and then not putting fuel in the tank.

If you do not have great natural beauty, one of the things you can do to make yourself attractive is to develop a beautiful mind.

As you get older, physical beauty tends to fade. But beauty of mind is independent of age and can actually increase with wisdom and experience.

Many people spend a great deal of time, effort and money to make themselves more physically beautiful. It makes sense to spend some time and effort to make your mind more beautiful.

What is beauty? Beauty is something that can be appreciated by others. The beautiful mind described in this book is a mind that can be appreciated by others. It is not the mind of a person who sits in a corner and solves very complex puzzles. It is a mind that can be appreciated by others – usually through conversation.

The beauty of your mind shows in your conversation. That is what this book is about. The beauty of your mind should show in your conversation. Just as people can look at your physical beauty they can listen to the beauty of your mind.

If you want to make your mind more beautiful you can. It is not a matter of innate intelligence or great knowledge. It is how you *use* your mind that matters. That is exactly what this book is about.

Edward de Bono

1 🌴 how to **agree**

To have a beautiful mind you must genuinely seek to find points of agreement with the person to whom you are talking. Surprisingly this is the most difficult aspect of all.

It is so difficult because the agreement must be genuine and not just sycophantic pretence. It is difficult because the motivation to do this is contrary to most people's natural inclinations.

We can look at two extremes of agreement and disagreement:

You are so right . . .
I agree with everything you say . . .
I completely agree with you . . .
Absolutely right . . .
I agree one hundred per cent . . .

If you agree with everything, there is not much of a discussion, not much of a conversation and not much of an exchange of views. The other person might as well be giving a lecture. Nice as it may sound, your contribution is not very significant.

Then there is the other extreme:

Yes, but . . .
I totally disagree . . .
You are wrong there . . .
That is not so . . .

This is the person who makes a point of disagreeing with everything that is said. This highly argumentative person seeks to demonstrate superiority through disagreement. Too often, academics or highly educated people behave in this manner because they have been encouraged to do so. This type of mind is intensely irritating and is far from being a beautiful mind.

You need to be somewhere between these two extremes. You do not have to agree with everything. You should not disagree with everything.

THE NEED TO BE RIGHT

This is very much tied up with the ego. An argument is a battle between egos. When you agree you seem to be submitting to the other point of view – so you lose. When you disagree you are asserting your ego and indicating that you may be superior. All this is reinforced by the emphasis on argument and debate in school and also in society, whether in government, the law courts or the media. In government, for instance, an opposition party will often seek to disagree with those in power, whatever the circumstances. Most people are now coming to see this as extremely silly.

If you insist on always winning an argument you end up with nothing more than you started with – except showing off your arguing ability. When you lose an argument you may well have gained a new point of view. Being right all the time is not the most important thing in the world and it is certainly not very beautiful.

> *A discussion should be a genuine attempt to explore a subject rather than a battle between competing egos.*

THE LOGIC BUBBLE

I created the term 'logic bubble' in a previous book. When someone does something you do not like or with which you do not agree, it is easy to label that person as stupid, ignorant or malevolent. But that person may be acting 'logically' within his or her 'logic bubble'. That bubble is made up of the perceptions, values, needs and experience of that person. If you make a real effort to see inside that bubble and to see where that person is 'coming from', you usually see the logic of that person's position.

In the school programme for teaching thinking (CoRT (Cognitive Research Trust) programme) there are tools which broaden perception so the thinker sees a wider picture and acts accordingly. One of these tools is OPV, which encourages the thinker to 'see the Other Person's Point of View'. We have numerous examples where a serious fight came to a sudden end when the combatants (who had learned the methods) decided to do an OPV on each other, a very similar process to understanding the 'logic bubble' of the other party.

SPECIAL CIRCUMSTANCES

This is the major way in which disagreement can be turned into agreement.

Someone makes a statement with which you immediately disagree. For example: 'Woman believe in psychics and fortune tellers more than men do.'

Your instant reaction is that this is untrue. It may be that women have more *fun* with fortune tellers even if they do not 'believe' in them. Women with somewhat dull lives may enjoy the new events offered. In the past women did not always have full control over their lives so they had to 'wait' for things to happen to them and the fortune teller would suggest events or incidents. When women had no political or military status, their only source of power was the occult. This meant that they developed the areas of sorcery and witchcraft because these gave power. Note the success of the Harry Potter books. Younger children who have little real influence enjoy the idea of wielding the power of wizardry and spells.

These are all special circumstances within which you might agree that some women do show more interest in psychics than do men.

In a different conversation, someone suggests that 'arranged marriages' are a good idea. Your immediate reaction is to disagree, because you believe in romance, love and free choice. Then you consider some special circumstances. In isolated communities the chance of meeting a suitable bride or groom might be slight. Relatives and a marriage broker might be better placed to identify potential couples.

A senior Indian business woman who had been educated at Columbia and Yale once told me: 'In the West you start off with love, violins in the sunset – and then it is downwards from then on. We start off in neutral and then we invest and make the relationship ever stronger. We have to try.'

So another special circumstance might be that both parties grow up in a culture where such betrothals are an expectation. You may also want to make a clear distinction between 'arranged' and 'forced' marriages.

In practice, you make an effort to find some special circumstances within which the statement does make sense and then you agree with the statement but only for those circumstances.

SPECIAL VALUES

Here you are saying: 'If I had those values, I would agree with you.'

This process is similar to the search for special circumstances. Instead of seeking the special circumstances you seek out the special values which would allow you to agree.

For example: 'Telling a lie is never acceptable. That is a moral principle.'

You can agree or disagree. As a matter of interest, philosophers over the ages have disagreed on this point. Some say that telling a lie is always wrong. Others say that you may tell a lie 'for the greater good'. Philosophers use the following traditional exaggeration: 'Suppose a murderer is pursuing a potential victim and asks you which way the victim has gone. Should you tell the murderer the correct or the incorrect way?'

Here we see a set of conflicting values: moral principles; pragmatism; value of human life.

So you spell out the different values and show that you would agree under one set of values but not under another set of values. You may still give your opinion.

SPECIAL EXPERIENCE

It is always difficult to argue with special experience. A person with years of experience looking after battered women may suggest that they often go back because their self-esteem is so low they need the relationship.

As a listener you may feel that they go back because they have nowhere else to go.

You can agree that in some instances the 'self-esteem' factor may be relevant, but not in all cases.

SWEEPING GENERALISATIONS

It is usually very difficult to agree with sweeping generalisations (see also page 21). Unfortunately, our logic habits demand that we think in this way: all crocodiles are vicious; all puppies are messy; no politician can be trusted; men are logical, women are intuitive.

The latter statement is exactly the sort of generalisation with which most people would disagree. But you can disagree with the generalisation as such and still agree with some aspects of it. For example: 'Women can be as logical as men when necessary but also tend to be more intuitive.'

Or: 'Men usually work in groups and logic is a way of convincing the other members of the group to go along with a plan. Women tend to act on their own and can rely on intuition as they do not need to persuade anyone else.'

Or: 'I agree that women do tend to have a more scanning mind that takes in more factors instead of just moving from one point to another.'

So, in this way, you can disagree with the sweeping generalisation but show agreement with some of the implications.

In real life there are many gradations between 'none' and 'all'. These might be:

none
a few
some
many
most
the majority
by and large
all

Unfortunately, our Greek-based logic system, with its inclusions and exclusions, cannot deal with such gradations. All fire burns, therefore this fire will burn you. No sand is good to eat, so do not eat this sand. This system has been wonderful in science and technology where properties are permanent, but much less useful in human affairs where there are interactive loops. The person you call an idiot is no longer the same person you called an idiot.

Dogmatism, rigidity, prejudice and bigotry all arise from this 'box type' thinking. Something is 'in the box' (and for ever) or 'outside the box' (and for ever). To be fair, this is very useful thinking and so we do have to use it. But the beautiful mind sees below the rigidity of the box structures and explores things in a more subtle way.

HOW TO AGREE **SUMMARY**

1 Genuinely seek to find points of agreement in what the other person is saying.

2 There is no contribution if you simply agree with everything.

3 To disagree at every point is irritating and boring.

4 Being argumentative is not at all beautiful. There are better methods of exploring a subject.

5 There is no need to be 'right' all the time. Remove your ego from the discussion and focus instead on the subject matter.

6 Make a real effort to see where the other person is coming from. Explore that person's 'logic bubble'.

7 See if there are any circumstances in which the other person's views might be right. Spell out such circumstances and show your agreement under those circumstances.

8 See if there are any special values which might make the other person's view valid. Show that under those values you would agree. But also have your own opinion.

9 Acknowledge the value of someone's special experience and treat this as a strong possibility but not necessarily complete.

10 Reject a sweeping generalisation but see whether you agree with any of the implications or any aspect of the generalisation.

11 Take a genuine delight in discovering points of
    agreement – even when there is overall
    disagreement.

12 Changing your perceptions to look at things in a
    different way is an important step in reaching
    possible agreement.

2 🌴 how to **disagree**

If you do not know how to disagree you will never have a beautiful mind. This is the critical operation. If you get this wrong then your mind will be ugly even if it is effective.

There are those who disagree in a rude and aggressive way.
There are those who disagree in order to do battle and to show they are winning.
There are those who disagree in order to vaunt their egos.
There are those who disagree in a bullying way.
There are those who disagree in order to demonstrate their superiority.
There are those who disagree because they have been taught that is what conversation is about.
There are those who disagree because they simply do not know any other way of exploring a subject.

A court of law is actually a rather primitive way of exploring a subject. If the prosecutor thinks of some point which would help the case for the defence, is the prosecutor going to bring that point forward? Of course not! If the defence attorney thinks of some point to strengthen the prosecution case, is he or she going to put that point forward? Of course not! Each side makes its own case, defends that case and attacks the case of the other side. This 'battle' does not mean that the matter is thoroughly examined. A much more effective way of exploring a subject is given by the use of 'parallel thinking' (see Chapter 8). With this method both parties jointly explore the subject.

Even though disagreement can be unpleasant, it is often necessary both for the sake of the truth and in order to investigate any issue objectively and fully.

POLITENESS

You are just stupid.
That is the silliest thing I have heard in a long time.
That is wrong.
That is poor logic.
I disagree with everything you have said.
How stupid can you be?

All these are rather harsh and rude ways of expressing disagreement. A better choice of expression can still communicate disagreement without being offensive:

I am not sure I follow your reasoning.
There might be another way of looking at it.

That is only one point of view.
How about this other possibility?
I think I have some doubts about your conclusion.
Maybe that is so, and maybe it is not so.
I can think of an alternative explanation.

Gentle disagreement is as valid as aggressive disagreement. On the whole, it is more beautiful to be gentle than to be aggressive.

There may be many different reasons for the disagreement. Some are listed here.

ERRORS OF LOGIC

Across Europe the number of people in prison ranges from 89 to 120 per hundred thousand of the population. In the USA the figure is more than six times as much at 750 per hundred thousand. Could this mean that the USA is less law abiding?

The conclusion does not necessarily follow from the statistics.

It may be that in the USA the police are better at catching
  criminals.
It may be that in the USA more types of crime are treated by
  prison sentences.
It may be that in the USA people stay longer in prison.

It may be that since 95 per cent of criminal cases in the USA are settled by plea bargaining, the number ending up in prison is higher.

By seeking such alternatives, you can show that the number of people in prison does not necessarily mean a greater amount of crime. That is just one possible explanation.

Someone might say: 'People do not like short politicians so they will not vote for Harris.' It may be true that, all things being equal, people prefer taller politicians. But things may not be equal. Mr Harris could have much more administrative experience than his rivals.

One thing may 'seem' to follow from another but you may disagree as to whether it 'has to' follow. You can challenge that necessity. If you can show a possible alternative, that makes your challenge much stronger.

INTERPRETATION

This is related to the previous source of error. One interpretation of statistics is given, and the impression is given that this interpretation is the only possible version. Yet there are other possible alternative explanations.

For example: In Sweden almost 50 per cent of babies are born to unmarried mothers. In Iceland the figure is 66 per cent. This might mean that marriage is not regarded very highly or that there are low moral standards, or that it represents a breakdown of families.

One other possible interpretation is that couples do not get married until there is a real 'baby-reason' for getting married. The statistics do not tell whether the couple eventually do get married after the baby is born.

To take another example, statistics in Australia show that people born under the Zodiac sign of Gemini are more likely to have car accidents than any other sign.

It is rather unlikely that the accident rate for all Zodiac signs would be exactly equal. So you would like to know whether this finding is significant across different periods and in different countries. The size of the difference would also be important.

One possible explanation is that those with a Gemini birthday reach the legal age for driving in winter (June in Australia) and so start driving in difficult conditions.

SELECTIVE PERCEPTION

A wife who finds out her husband is having an affair looks back over the whole marriage and picks out only those points which suggest that the husband does not truly love her.

Selective perception means perceiving things in such a way as to support a pre-formed idea.

The classic use of selective perception is with stereotypes and prejudices. The mind has a fixed pattern and then notices only those things which fit the pattern. Racial prejudice is an obvious example.

A fierce feminist would be ready to pick on any male behaviour evidence to indicate male chauvinism.

Selective perception can work both ways. For instance: At one time 50 per cent of the employees at NASA were Indian and 26 per cent of the employees at Microsoft were also Indian.

This might suggest that Indians were especially intelligent or skilled at computer work. There is a big software industry in India (around Bangalore) and there are good training institutes for computer work. So Indians going to the USA were likely to end up in such jobs. In addition the shortage of IT specialists in the USA meant that the USA gave special visas to Indians with these skills.

Selective perception is difficult to challenge because what is said may be correct. The listener has no way of knowing what has *not* been said, or has been left out. A person who tells you all the instances where an employee seems to have been lazy may choose not to tell you all the instances where the same person worked exceptionally hard.

If you believe that a certain race commits more crimes, you will only notice instances of that race committing crimes. You may not see that crime occurs more often in certain economic groups and there happen to be more of that race in these groups.

EMOTIONS

Emotions follow on from prejudice and stereotypes.

Is the person really giving an objective view or is there an emotional tinge to it? It is usually very easy to tell the emotional content by the adjectives used. (See also page 141.)

Adjectives such as lazy, useless, dishonest, careless, dangerous, devious and shifty immediately suggest that an opinion is very much emotional. If you strip the adjectives from the opinion then the opinion collapses. The opinion is therefore just a vehicle for the emotions.

Everyone is free to express their emotions. A listener, however, does not have to be persuaded by the emotions or to agree with them. It is when emotions enter the logic of an opinion that they become dangerous. If emotions are clearly labelled as such, there is no danger: 'This is what I feel about the matter.'

The listener may still ask why these emotions are in place.

Emotions can be reactions to events. Emotions can also determine the way the events are perceived.

DIFFERENT EXPERIENCE

In Chapter 3 it is pointed out that different personal experiences lead to different opinions. The same holds for disagreement. If your personal experience differs from the speaker's personal experience, you may well find yourself disagreeing with the conclusions put forward by the speaker.

A person who lives in a country that has a monarchy may have a very different experience from someone who lives in a country without royalty. A person who has gone through a divorce will have a different experience from someone who has never been divorced.

Having a different experience never means that your experience is the right one and the experience of the other party is invalid. In disagreeing, you simply point out that your experience is different: 'My experience in working with young offenders is obviously not the same as yours. I found that . . .'

Once again there is both different experience and also different interpretation of experience. For instance:

As a young doctor, I found that the nursing staff took very good care of the patients.

As a young doctor, I found that the nursing staff had little time for the patients.

At first, the two sets of experience seem contradictory. It then turns out that in the second case the hospital was understaffed and the nurses were overworked, therefore seeming to have little time for the patients.

SWEEPING GENERALISATIONS

In general there should always be a tendency to disagree with sweeping generalisations, as discussed in Chapter 1 (see page 9).

The very nature of generalisations means that the same label applies to everyone or everything that is placed in the labelled box: all children are cute; all lawyers are argumentative; all Italians are romantic; all Frenchwomen are marvellous cooks.

As a challenge to such sweeping generalisations you might suggest whether the words 'many' or 'most' would do as well as 'all'. If such words will not do because they destroy the logic of the argument, then you need to doubt that logic – at least where it applies to people. In technical areas, generalisations may indeed apply.

EXTRAPOLATIONS

There is a joke about the airline pilot who apologised to the passengers for having to shut down one engine. He explained that it meant they would arrive two hours late into New York. A second engine failed and he explained that they would be four hours late. Then a third engine failed. At this point the co-pilot leaned across to him and said: 'I hope to goodness the last engine does not fail or we shall be up here all night!'

Extrapolation means taking a trend forward and assuming the trend will continue. Ecologists have to do this all the time in their warnings about global warming, for example. Sometimes they may be right and sometimes they may be wrong.

The number of students entering tertiary education is rising in most countries. Can we extrapolate that to a world in which everyone has tertiary education and there are not enough suitable jobs to go around? The Chinese economy is growing at 8 per cent a year (much faster than most other countries). Can we extrapolate that to make China the dominant economic power in the world?

Like sweeping generalisations, extrapolations need to be treated with caution. There may be some element of truth in them but they are unlikely to work out as claimed. Very often, counter forces come in which oppose the trend.

POSSIBLE AND CERTAIN

This is one of the most important points about disagreement.

You may be willing to accept something as a 'possibility' but very unwilling to accept it as a 'certainty'.

It is *possible* that raising the school leaving age will reduce juvenile crime. It would be difficult to accept this as a certainty.

It is *possible* that the higher suicide rate among men after the break-up of a relationship is due to the break-up being more of a surprise to men than it is to women.

There is a whole spectrum between 'just possible' and 'certain':

just possible
possible
likely
very likely
probable
most probable
certain

When disagreeing with something that has been put forward as a certainty, you can indicate the level of 'possible' at which you are prepared to accept the statement. For example:

It is possible that China may become a dominant economic power in the next fifty years.
It is just possible that a human colony will be established on the moon or a planet.
It is very likely that HIV will become the major problem in Africa.

DIFFER OR DISAGREE

Disagreement implies a regard for the truth. There is a truth concern. You do not want to let someone get away with something which is either untrue or offered as true without being proved to be so.

In the spaghetti metaphor used in Chapter 3 (see page 27), the range of different sauces is a matter of choice. If someone suggested sprinkling ground coffee on the spaghetti, you would probably reject that as plain 'wrong'. (In fact, I have tried this and it works very well!) If, however, someone suggested using diesel fuel on the spaghetti you would certainly reject this – not only in terms of taste but it may also be poisonous.

So in disagreement you may be implying one of several things:

That is simply wrong
That is possible but not certain
That is only one of many alternatives
That fits your experience
That fits your values
That is right for you but not for me
That is based on emotions and prejudice
That is based on selective perception
The conclusion does not follow
That is one possible view of the future

This wide range of types of disagreement should, as far as possible, be indicated and spelled out. It is too abrupt simply to say that you disagree. The method of disagreement does need to be indicated.

Once this is done the disagreement can be explored.

HOW TO DISAGREE **SUMMARY**

1 Do not disagree for the sake of disagreeing.

2 Do not disagree just to show how clever you are or to boost your ego.

3 When you disagree, do so politely and gently rather than rudely and aggressively.

4 You may need to disagree to point out that a fact or statement is simply wrong.

5 You may need to point out errors of logic or to show that a conclusion does not necessarily follow from what went before.

6 You may need to point out selective perception and particular interpretations of statistics or events.

7 Where emotions, prejudices and stereotypes appear to be used, you may want to indicate this.

8 You may want to disagree to show a different personal experience.

9 Almost always you will want to challenge sweeping generalisations.

10 You will want to challenge conclusions based on extreme extrapolations into the future.

11 It is very important to challenge 'certainty' and to suggest 'possibility' instead.

12 Distinguish between having a different opinion and disagreeing with an opinion.

3 🌴 how to **differ**

Actors audition to get parts in a play. Quite often the actor gets turned down. Being turned down a number of times is very discouraging and the actor tends to lose self-confidence. So their agents tell them: 'You are an apple. They are looking for oranges. This does not mean you are a bad actor or a bad apple. They simply want something different.'

Some people like spaghetti with a puttanesca sauce. Some people prefer an arrabiata sauce and some like a traditional Neapolitan. These are all different but there is no suggestion that one is better than the other.

Children in a family can be different from each other but may all be equally loved by their parents.

TWO SORTS OF DIFFERENCE

Surprising as it may seem, it is said that in the dark most people would be unable to distinguish between whisky and cognac. So, in the dark, a glass is handed around and players in the game are asked to guess what is in the glass. Some people say it is whisky, others say it is cognac. The opinions differ. But there is only one truth, or correct answer. What is in the glass is either whisky or cognac and not both. So the opinions differ but only one set of opinions is 'right'.

'What is this?' There may be differences of opinion but at best only one will be right (they may all be wrong). So there is the type of difference where one opinion is right and other opinions are not right.

There is, however, another sort of difference. Consider the following two statements:

If we raise the selling price of the magazine, fewer people will want to buy it and we shall lose money.

If we raise the selling price of the magazine, people will regard it as a more prestigious magazine and we may even get more readers – in addition to the extra revenue from the sales.

Whenever we look forward into the future, it is always possible to have different opinions about what might happen. It is very difficult in foresight to tell which opinion is 'right'. There may, in some cases, be research or precedents to suggest which opinion may turn out to be correct. Usually, however, the future is open to differences of opinion.

SOURCES OF DIFFERENCE

This food needs more salt.
This food has enough salt.

Differences may arise from personal preferences. Some
people like horror movies. Some people like 'bang-bang'
movies. Some like Westerns. There is enough difference
in personal taste to enable most people to marry a partner
of their choice.

Let us imagine that two people are arguing over the
best way to get from A to B.

'It would be best to go through the village of
Clickford,' says one.

'Using the turnpike would be a better bet,' says the other.

It all depends on what is meant by 'best way'. There are
several possible meanings:

best means the fastest route
best means the most scenic route
best means the easiest route to follow
best means the route with least traffic
best means the shortest route

Unless 'best' is clearly defined, the differences of opinion
are all valid. It may be that for one person the easiest
route to follow is the best. For another person the fastest
route is best. And so on.

Envisage a person standing to the north of a church, who describes the church from that point of view. Another person is standing to the south of the church and describes the church from that point of view. Both views are valid views of the church. They are different but both are valid.

There is the story of a man who painted half his car white and the other half black. His friends asked him why he had done this strange thing. He replied:

'When I have an accident, it is such fun hearing the witnesses in court contradict each other. One witness claims it was a white car which knocked the cyclist over. Another witness, also under oath, claims that it was actually a black car.'

Both witness would be right – given their different points of view.

From the point of views of people who have to borrow money for business or mortgages, a low interest rate is a good thing. From the point of view of those who lend money or who live on the income from savings, a low interest rate is not a good thing at all. There is a strong difference of opinion, but both opinions are correct.

A different point of view will give a different perception. Even from the same point of view, however, there can be differences of perception.

From a parent's point of view the use of computers in school enables the children to access a vast range of information that would otherwise be inaccessible. From a parent's point of view computers reduce the social interaction between youngsters and so limit their social experience and the ability to get on with others. Both perceptions are from the same (parent's) point of view. Both are valid. Yet they are different.

In another example, the pessimist looks at a glass half filled with wine and claims it is 'half empty'. The optimist looks at it and says it is 'half full'. The re-engineering consultant looks at it and claims 'there is too much glass'. The wine maker looks at it and notes that it is 'red wine'.

As suggested in the chapter on agreement, different values will always lead to a difference of opinion.

When the US government suggested giving child benefits to babies still in the womb, different values led to a difference of opinion. There were those who welcomed the acknowledgement that pregnant women had extra needs due to the child they were carrying so it was logical to give much needed assistance. There were those who saw the move as a way to discourage abortion because the unborn child had been declared to be a human being. It might also mean that abortions could now be reported and recorded.

When more and more students achieved higher grades in school-leaving examinations in the UK, there were those who welcomed the fact that more pupils were now getting good grades which might help them in the job market. There were others, however, who lamented the 'dumbing down' of the examinations and who asked for a new superior grade so the elite of the cleverest could still be picked out.

Differences are also based on differing experiences. A teacher teaching in an economically deprived area will have experiences different from those of a teacher in a more affluent area.

For example, we find that the direct teaching of 'thinking' as a skill in schools (see also page 6) has a marked effect on self-esteem and behaviour in deprived areas. Youngsters now feel able to take control of their lives and to make decisions, choices and plans. In affluent areas the effect is more on the school work than on behaviour.

The experience of a person coming out of a bad marriage will differ from that of a person in a good marriage.

I remember one young Australian woman, Katie, telling me that in an ideal marriage the wife should adore the husband and he should appreciate that. Whenever I quote that to other people there is a wide difference in response: 'It should be the other way around'; or 'It should be equally balanced'. These differences arise from direct personal experience – a good or bad marriage, perhaps; from experience within a family; and from the experiences of others (as read in magazines, for instance).

There can be a huge difference with regard to views of the future. No one can be sure about the future. We can get some idea about the future from the past and from research. At best these only give some indications of what might happen – a guess. Personal experience and experience within a field will also help to form ideas about the future.

Suppose there was a suggestion that marriage should be a formal five-year contract, which could be renewed at the end of five years if both parties so wished. There would also need to be provision for any children born during the five years. What would happen? What would happen to society? What would happen to men and to women? What would happen to the children?

The 'judgement' as to whether this was a sound suggestion or not would depend on personal values and experience. The judgement, however, could only be applied if you, personally, looked into the future. You have to imagine the possible consequences before you can judge the value of the suggestion. There might be many possibilities. The outcome would not be uniform. Some might be affected for the better, some for the worse. It could be argued that those in a happy marriage would simply renew the contract. Those in a poor marriage would have a simple way out. Others might envisage irresponsible people going through a series of marriages.

SPELL OUT THE DIFFERENCE

The most important thing to do about differences of opinion is to spell out as clearly as possible the actual difference. For example:

I think that raising prices will increase sales. You think that raising prices will reduce sales.

I believe that 'thinking' can be taught directly as a skill in school. You believe that you cannot teach thinking directly but can only pick up good thinking habits through studying other subjects.

You believe that severe punishment is the best way to control crime in all cases. I believe that giving youngsters an alternative way of sensing achievement will reduce crime amongst the young.

Lay out the differing opinions alongside each other. Seek to be as honest as you can about this. Get the other person to agree that you have spelled out the point of difference correctly. If necessary, invite the other person to summarise the point of difference as he or she sees it.

Try to reach the point where you can say: 'We agree to differ on this point.'

SPELL OUT THE REASONS FOR
THE DIFFERENCE

Having laid out the nature of the 'difference', the next step is to try to lay out the reason for the difference:

I believe that you are looking at it from that point of view . . .
    and I am looking at it from this point of view . . . (and
    give the two different points of view).
We are looking at it in two different ways. This is my
    perception . . . and I believe your perception to be
    . . . (and give the two perceptions).
The difference may just arise from personal preference. You
    like clever people and I prefer charming people.
We are using different sets of values. My values are as
    follows . . . Your values seem to be . . . (and lay out the
    differing values).
The difference may arise from differing personal experience.
    My experience has been . . . Your experience may have
    been different (give your personal experience).
We seem to have different views about what might happen in
    the future. My view is based on . . . Your view seems to be
    different (give some basis for your view of the future).

ACCEPT THE DIFFERENCE

Before accepting the difference, an attempt should be made to reconcile the difference.

Sometimes it can be shown that both opinions are valid but they apply to different parts of the situation. For instance: 'I accept that for many types of crime severe punishment is the best deterrent but for youth crime I think there is another approach: give youngsters other opportunities for achievement.'

This is very similar to the suggestions made in Chapter 1 (How to Agree).

It might be shown that both parties are not really looking at the same thing. In the case of the half-empty wine glass, one person is looking at the empty space and the other person is looking at the remaining wine.

As in the example of the 'best route' from A to B, a clear definition of what is 'best' can often reconcile differences of opinion. An opinion is a sort of judgement. What is the basis for that judgement? Are we looking to see if something is good for society in general, or just for me?

Differences of personal experience can be jointly explored. It may be that the experience is valid but the interpretation of the experience is not necessarily the only one. Maybe youngsters in deprived areas do commit more crime and not because of economic needs but because they have to relate more to a gang than to their family – and gangs have to have activity.

Differences of opinion about the future can be explored by looking at parallel situations, such as: 'When they raised the price of that perfume, sales actually increased.'

There may be precedents. Some of them may be more valid than others. Raising the price of a perfume may not be the same as raising the price of a magazine.

Research and further information may help sort out differences about the future. There is no way of being certain about the future. But some guesses are more likely than others. The intention is to work together to try to forecast the future.

Having made a genuine effort to reconcile the different opinions, there may be 'an agreement to disagree'. This may take the form of an agreement that with different priorities or different sets of values, opinions will inevitably differ. At least the basis for the difference will be clear to all parties.

Difference of opinion is not a bad thing. Difference enriches the situation. Clarification of different values and experiences adds to the discussion. The intention is not to 'remove' the difference because difference is bad, but to investigate a subject through exploring the basis for the difference.

There is nothing worse than a 'hidden' difference where both parties think they are discussing the same thing from the same point of view with the same values and experience – and this is not so at all. The fiercest and the stupidest of arguments usually arise in this manner.

This is like the witnesses in court arguing whether the accident was caused by a white car or a black car. It would never have occurred to them that a single car could be both black and white at the same time!

HOW TO DIFFER **SUMMARY**

1 There are times when only one of a different set of opinions can be right. This is where 'truth' can be checked out.

2 More often different opinions can all have their own validity.

3 Difference may arise from a different definition of the basis for judgement (the 'best' road).

4 Difference may arise from personal preference, taste or choice.

5 Difference may arise from a different set of values.

6 Difference may arise from a different point of view or perspective.

7 Difference may arise from a different perception even if from the same point of view.

8 Difference may arise from differing personal experience or differing knowledge.

9 Difference may arise from a different view of possible futures.

10 Seek to lay out as clearly as possible the nature of the difference. Lay one opinion alongside the different one.

11 Seek to explore and explain the reasons for the difference.

12 Seek to reconcile the differences and then agree to differ on what cannot be reconciled.

4 how to be **interesting**

Being interesting is much more important than winning an argument.

Being interesting is much more important than showing how clever you are.

If you are interesting people will want to be with you. People will seek your company. People will enjoy talking to you.

You may be interesting because you have taken part in an expedition to a remote part of the Amazon to meet up with a tribe that had never seen a white man before.

You may be interesting because you have sailed single-handedly around the world.

You may be interesting because you are carrying out fascinating DNA research on the population migrations in the history of humanity.

But for the sake of this book we shall assume that you have not done or are doing anything so spectacular. This is a little unfair because whatever you are doing, no matter how humble, is capable of being interesting.

The first rule is to talk about what you are good at and what interests you. It may be your job or it may be your hobby. You will need to fashion your discourse to suit two different audiences. The first is made up of those who know nothing about the subject. It is up to you to present the subject in an interesting manner. The second type of audience is made up of those who know something about the matter and want to know more. In the latter case you should invite questions and seek to answer them.

INFORMATION

Did you know that female stick insects can have baby girl stick insects without any need for a male at all? If we could work out the hormonal combination that triggered the cells to divide then feminists could really get rid of men.

The seahorse may be the most feminist of all creatures. The female produces the egg, which the male fertilises. The female then 'hands' the fertilised egg to the male who has to look after it until the babies hatch.

In Queensland, Australia, there is a frog that swallows its eggs which have been fertilised by the male frog. The frog then turns off the hydrochloric acid and digestive juices in its stomach. The eggs develop in the frog's stomach. When the young frogs are mature, the mother frog opens its mouth and the babies just hop out.

Unusual information is one type of interest. You can accumulate such information by remembering paragraphs you have read in newspapers or magazines. You can also take a special interest in some exotic matter and really become an expert: Zulu wars; yacht design; or family structure in Kazakhstan.

For the moment, however, let us suppose that you have no special information and are not doing anything very special. How then can you be interesting?

WHAT IF?

What if dogs could be taught to speak? What would happen?

It would be hard to keep family secrets because your dog would tell the neighbour's dog and so on around the community.

Your dog could answer back. If you told your dog to go outside the dog might ask: 'Why should I?' Your dog could also indicate whether it liked the food it was given and when it was hungry.

You could set your dog to work: to answer the phone and to carry out errands. Your dog might ask a burglar: 'Excuse me, what are you doing here?'

Single children and older people on their own would have a friend they could talk to.

Dogs might want political rights and even votes.

Television and other advertising would take into account the fact that dogs could listen to the advertisements and that dogs could now influence their masters.

Dogs might work for newspapers as reporters using voice recognition software to type out their stories.

What if China became the dominant economic power in the world?

What if women had to propose marriage?

What if human cloning became available and relatively cheap?

What if the HIV level in the USA reached the level in parts of Africa?

What if subliminal techniques made TV advertising extremely powerful?

What if we all began to speak in code instead of ordinary language?

What if everyone read this book?

The 'what if?' approach involves playing with ideas. Since the ideas are to be played out in the future, there is no way of checking which will happen and which will not. Because it is so open-ended, an effort should be made to put forward ideas that are as 'logical' as possible. For the sake of humour, the occasional 'fantasy' might be allowed.

Using this playful approach, the simplest of situations can be turned into an interesting game. For example: What if chief executives were to be trained as chief executives from the youngest age – as soon as they entered the corporation?

In France, judges are trained as judges from the earliest age. In the UK successful barristers are chosen and asked to become judges, although they often decline because the drop in income may be huge.

POSSIBILITIES AND ALTERNATIVES

Most conversation and argument strives towards certainty: 'this is the way it is'; 'this is not right'; 'this is what should (or should not) happen'.

Putting forward alternatives and other possibilities can make the discussion more interesting. The possibilities can then be explored – even if they are finally rejected. For instance: Maybe tax could be handled in a different way. The taxpayer could decide with up to half the tax being paid what that money should be used for – health, education, defence. This would allow a sort of voting through taxation.

Alternative solutions could be offered for recognised problems or conflict situations. Once the solution has been offered then it can be discussed and considered.

Around 150,000 people have been killed in the conflict in Algiers. About 56,000 people have been killed in the war in Sri Lanka. Around 39,000 people have been killed in the fighting in Colombia. Could there be any better approaches to solving these sorts of conflicts (also Kashmir, Northern Ireland, Israel, etc.). Could the UN function in a different way?

A young Australian doctor suggested that peptic ulcers might be caused by an infection. At first everyone laughed at him. It turned out that he was right. People who had spent years on antacids could now be cured in a fortnight. Serious operations to remove part or all of the stomach (Billroth operations) were now no longer necessary. Science advances through hypotheses and alternative possibilities.

It is said that in the USA 75 per cent of people marry someone with whom they work. This seems a very limited choice. What other alternatives could there be: the Internet, newspaper columns, agencies, marriage brokers?

In Roman Catholic countries official suicide rates seem very low. Is this because a strong religious element reduces suicides or because a suicide cannot be buried in a church graveyard so suicides are not recorded as such?

Quite recently the lowest birthrate in Europe was in Spain, which is a Roman Catholic country that forbids contraceptive devices. What was happening?

Fat people often seem happy. Is this just an illusion? Is it that the same hormones that make them fat also make them happy? Do they eat more because they are happy? Do they seem happy because they see that as the only way they can contribute to society?

Once you get into the habit of looking for alternatives and possibilities, any subject becomes more interesting.

SPECULATION

I once knew a very famous philosopher. We were good friends but we found it difficult to hold a conversation because we each had a different view of what a conversation should be.

His idea of a conversation was that you should start out by defining your terms precisely. Then, at the end of the conversation, you would see whether or not the conclusions matched those initial definitions.

My idea of a conversation was more like climbing a 'chimney' in rock climbing. Each step took you further and further into new possibilities and new ideas. These could only be speculative. At the end you had a garden full of new plants.

Far too many people believe that thinking and talking should only be about the 'truth'. It may be correct that we should only trust and act upon the truth but in order to get there we may have to explore possibilities (as with a scientific hypothesis).

In conversation there is also the entertainment value. Speculation also has a much higher entertainment value than truth. Playing around with ideas is both interesting and entertaining.

Are there fewer women artists than men because women are more serious and have to get on with the serious business of life and families, while men can be more irresponsible, frivolous and self-indulgent?

CONNECTIONS

Making connections involves possibilities, alternatives and speculation. Is there a connection between the high suicide rate in China amongst women and the 'one child family' policy?

Was there a connection between the very successful organising of the 1984 Olympic Games in Los Angeles by Peter Ueberroth and the talk I gave to the Young Presidents Organisation in 1975 in Boca Raton? According to Peter Ueberroth there was and he used the creative techniques of lateral thinking to help him design the new concepts that made such a success of the Games.

Is there any connection between teenage pregnancy in England and a welfare policy that allocates public housing to mothers?

It is easy to see connections where there are none. Conspiracy theories and paranoia abound in imagined sinister connections. On the other hand, there is no harm in exploring possible connections so long as they are not taken seriously until proven.

CREATIVITY AND NEW IDEAS

If you are marking examination papers and one of the candidates puts forward a new idea, then that candidate moves ahead of all others. All the others may be very competent – but rather dull. A new idea shines out as being different.

It is the same in conversation. Most people can be reasonable and competent and rather dull. New ideas are rare because we have been taught analysis and judgement but never creativity.

There is a silly myth that creativity is a sort of mystical talent which some people have and which others can only envy. It is nothing of the sort. The main purpose of the brain is to allow incoming information to form itself into routine patterns. If the brain did not do this, life would be impossibly complicated and slow. So we identify situations and apply the routine pattern. This is the opposite of creativity. Instead of waiting for creative inspiration there should be some thinking methods which we could learn and use deliberately.

That is why I invented 'lateral thinking' with its formal methods. The term is now in most dictionaries and the methods are widely used in business and elsewhere. The methods include provocation, concept extraction, and random entry. All of them are based on an understanding of the behaviour of 'self-organising systems'. A self-organising system is one in which information arranges itself into patterns. A provocation is a statement which we know to be false, but use to provoke new ideas by 'moving forward' from the statement. In any self-organising information system there is a mathematical need for provocation. I created the word 'po' to signal that what followed was a provocation.

Take, for instance, a factory on a river, which emitted pollution. People downstream suffered from this pollution. The following provocation, 'Po, the factory is downstream of itself', seems impossible and illogical. But from the provocation comes a perfectly practical idea. If you build a factory on a river then your input must always be downstream of your own output – so you have to be more concerned about cleaning up your own pollution. I am told this has since become legislation in some countries.

'Po, people should decide, in advance, their own date of death.'

This was a provocation I used at a meeting of Nobel prize economists who were discussing pension schemes.

Creativity is a skill and a habit. You need to learn and practise the skill, which then becomes a habit. But even without any special creative skill you can always seek to have new ideas and to put them forward. If nothing else, the new idea will provide a starting point for fresh considerations.

A MOST USEFUL HABIT

You need to get into the habit of saying: 'Now that is interesting.'

Once you are ready to use that phrase you can now direct the phrase at anything that comes up in the conversation. So instead of just carrying on with the flow of the conversation you now pause at that point. You explore the point. You elaborate around the point. You open up possibilities and alternatives. You make connections.

It is like having a bow and a quiver full of arrows. At any moment you aim your arrow at a particular point and let fly: 'Now that is interesting!'

You will need to explain why you find that point interesting. You will need to build up and lay out the interesting aspects. You invite the other party to join you in exploring the point.

You should learn to use the phrase very formally as an attention-directing tool. It is not enough just to wait for the attitude to arise. You need to 'direct attention' in a deliberate manner (see also page 77).

EXERCISES

Being interested and being interesting go together. You need to develop the habit of finding interest in almost anything. Developing this habit of mind needs practice. A very simple way of doing this is to take different things and then to seek to find interest in them. Imagine you were talking about these subjects. What would you say? How could you be interesting about each of the following?

frogs
democracy
airports
chewing gum
flags
steering wheels
advertising
royalty
scrambled eggs

Try this simple exercise by yourself or with others. Cut out pieces of card and write different words (like the above) on separate pieces and put them into a bag. Without looking, draw a single card out of the bag. Everyone then tries to find something 'interesting' to say about that item.

HOW TO BE INTERESTING **SUMMARY**

1   It is always important to get to the truth, but being
    interesting is more important than winning an
    argument. You owe it to yourself and to others to be
    interesting.

2   Interest may arise from interesting things you have
    done, are doing or know about. Interest can also
    arise from how you conduct a conversation.

3   Using the 'what if?' technique can open up new
    possibilities and new lines of thought.

4   Looking out for possibilities and alternatives
    enriches the conversation. There is usually more
    than one way of doing things or looking at things.

5   Speculation looks forward and opens up new areas
    of interest. Description only looks backward.

6   Finding and making connections links matters
    together and generates interest.

7   New ideas are rare and freshen any discussion. Seek
    to be creative and to generate new ideas. Learn and
    apply the formal techniques of lateral thinking.

8   Provocation is a useful way to force new ideas. You
    put forward a statement you know to be wrong or
    impossible in order to provoke new thinking.

9   Use as a formal tool the phrase: 'Now that is
    interesting.' Be ready to apply this to anything you hear.

10 Seek to explore and elaborate and to pull interest
    out of any matter.

11 Practise simple exercises to develop your ability to
    create interest.

12 When someone else opens up an interesting line of
    thought, go along with it and help to develop the
    interest further.

5 🌴 how to **respond**

In general, the main objectives in any discussion, discourse or conversation could be summarised as follows:

To reach agreement. This may be because both parties are seeking truth or because they have to design a practical way forward for action.

To spell out and agree on the points of difference. This also includes spelling out the basis for the difference – values, experience or point of view, for instance.

To have as interesting a time as possible in the course of the discussion.

Those are the overall strategies or objectives. Getting there involves many other activities which happen from moment to moment. That is what this chapter is about. What is the immediate reaction, reply or response to something that has been put forward?

Some of the basic responses have been covered in preceding chapters.

You can agree with what has been said. You might agree completely. You might agree partially. You can agree with a modification of what has been proposed.

You can differ with what has been said. You need to show exactly where you differ, how you differ and why you differ. The other party needs to know the exact nature of your difference.

You can disagree with what has been said. You can disagree with facts, with values, with experience, with conclusions and with 'certainty'. Once again you need to show the point of disagreement and the reasons for the disagreement.

You can suggest alternatives and possibilities, either to the whole proposition or to some part of it.

You can indicate a point of 'interest' and then seek to open up that point of interest.

You can summarise and then repeat back what you think you heard.

All these aspects have been considered in previous chapters and will also be revisited in future chapters.

This chapter is concerned with other aspects of a response.

CLARIFICATION

There are few things more silly than two people arguing at cross purposes because each has misunderstood what the other person is saying. This is a waste of energy. So if there is the slightest doubt, you need to ask for clarification:

Is this what you said . . .
I understood you to say this . . . Is that correct?
I am not sure I understood what you said. Could you
repeat it?
I am not totally clear about what you have just said.
Could you clarify it for me?

Any speaker wants to communicate and to be understood, so no one minds being asked to repeat or to clarify something. To ask for a clarification does not mean that you are stupid. On the contrary, you are showing so much interest in what is being said that you want to be sure you have understood it correctly.

In asking for a clarification you can simply ask the person to repeat, perhaps in simpler terms, what has already been said, or you can give your version and ask whether this is indeed correct.

'I understand you to be saying . . . Is that really what you are saying?'

SUPPORT

Support goes much further than simple agreement. Agreement can be signalled with a mere nod of the head or the word 'yes'.

generalisation that 'all teenagers are lazy' can be reduced to 'some teenagers seem lazy'.

Apart from the liveliness and 'actuality' of stories, they illustrate possibility. A teacher told how a schoolyard bully was totally transformed by the direct teaching of 'thinking' as a skill (not just critical thinking). I saw his letter to the teacher. In it he wrote: 'I used to think I was good at nothing, now I know I am good at thinking.' (And he was.)

Such a story does not 'prove' anything but it illustrates a possibility. The possibility is that youngsters who are not good at the usual school subjects are not stupid at all but potentially good thinkers. Once they realise this their self-esteem rises and they no longer need to be bullies.

Stories can illustrate principles – which is why there are the parables in the Bible.

Someone once told me about some complex calculations to see how much rocket fuel had been loaded. One day someone suggested putting in a window so that they could see the level of the fuel. The principle is that there may be a simpler and more direct way of doing things.

In Miletus, in ancient Greece, there was an epidemic of suicides. Young women heard that a friend of theirs had committed suicide and they proceeded to do the same. The hysteria was stopped by an old fellow in the Senate who introduced a law that the body of every suicide would be carried, naked, through the marketplace. There are many principles to be extracted from this story. One of them is the importance of vanity.

Examples from personal experience are particularly powerful. When I was a young Rhodes scholar at Oxford you were supposed to be back in college by a certain time. If you went off to a party in London and got back late you had to climb into the college. One foggy night I returned late from London. I knew that there were two walls to be climbed. So I climbed the two walls. I found myself outside again. In the fog I had climbed in and out across a corner. So when you are sure you are doing the obvious and correct thing, it is still worth checking!

There is a story about packers in a factory that used old newspapers in the packing process. The trouble was that the workers would spend too much time reading interesting bits in the old newspapers. They solved the problem (so it is said) by employing blind packers.

It is important to remember that stories do not prove anything. So a string of powerful stories does not prove a point. The stories illustrate matters and also show possibilities.

BUILD UPON

You may like the point that is being made. Not only do you agree and want to provide supporting material, but you actually want to 'build upon' the point.

Suppose someone is talking about 'the need for achievement in youngsters'. In support of this point you can offer the statistic that in the USA, 94 per cent of youngsters rated achievement as the most important thing in their lives.

This is support. Then you build upon the point and try to see where youngsters could get their sense of achievement. If a youngster was not gifted in the academic or sporting areas and did not play the guitar, where was achievement to come from? One possible area was 'hobbies'. Maybe a much more serious effort could be made to encourage and develop hobbies at school?

Someone else might be talking about how important self-esteem is to teenagers. You agree and then build upon this by offering a new idea. Suppose a rule, or suggestions, was in place that required all school principals to 'say something positive' about every child graduating from schools. Maybe the youngster was kind, or friendly, or on time, or helpful, or made people laugh. This would mean that teachers would start to look out for positive aspects outside the academic requirements.

EXTEND

An idea is suggested. You not only accept the idea but try to extend it.

The person putting forward the idea may not realise the full possibilities of the idea, so you help that person see these possibilities. Once again, this goes much further than mere agreement. There is a co-operative effort to get the most from the idea.

In the Veneto region of northern Italy there is said to be one business for every eleven people. The region is one of the most economically successful in the whole of the European Union. What is the secret of setting up small businesses?

One of the problems is risk. Someone suggests that low-interest loans (which are used in Italy) would help people to set up their own business. You can extend this attempt to reduce risk by suggesting another idea. When a small business collapses, the losses can be sold as a tax credit to any other company (which does not have to be in the same field). This removes some of the downside of setting up a small business.

CARRY FORWARD

This is really a version of the 'what if' process.

You take the suggested idea and then 'carry it forward' into practice and into the future.

It is suggested that in an election each voter should have both a positive vote and a negative vote. The negative vote would be used 'against' a candidate and would mean: 'I really do not want that person in government.'

You imagine the idea in practice. It might be difficult for extremists or tyrants to get into power. Their supporters would vote for them but everyone else would give them negative votes, which would then cancel the positive votes. A negative effect might be that people in one party would give negative votes to the most able person in the other party.

Carrying something forward means looking at all the possible consequences and scenarios. It is a genuine exploration – not just a search for aspects which support a point of view.

I once suggested that in the Middle East, Tuesday would be declared a violence-free day. This would mean that people could relax on Tuesday and would look forward to Tuesday. Then they would start to ask why every day was not like Tuesday and the impetus for peace would be increased. There is also a precedent for the idea. In the time of Muhammad, one day in the week was declared 'war free' and on that day you bought and sold camels and carried out other business.

In all these suggestions there is the spirit of co-operative exploration rather than an argument 'battle'.

MODIFY

You can offer to modify a proposition that is put forward. You may want to modify it to remove parts you do not like and so make the proposition more acceptable to you. You may modify the proposition to remove faults and weaknesses that occur to you. You may modify the proposition to make it even stronger.

One of the simplest forms of modification is to seek to reduce a sweeping generalisation to a less absolute statement (see also pages 9 and 21). For example: All sex offenders should be castrated.

This might be modified to: There may be a place for investigating hormonal treatment of some sex offenders.

I once put forward an interesting idea in Northern Ireland. The suggestion was that when a political party lost an election, those who had voted for the losing party would pay 10 per cent less income tax. The logic is that if the winning voters were to be governed by their choice of government, the losers would be compensated by paying less tax! There would need, however, to be voter registration. The idea was not well received because the Unionists, who generally formed the majority of the assembly, did not see why others should be compensated.

Now that idea could well be modified to make it more practical and more acceptable. The level of tax difference could be altered. The system might only be used if the same party had been in power for more than two terms.

It is not a matter of 'your idea' and 'my idea'. Once an idea has surfaced then it is there to be jointly developed and improved. Both parties benefit from that.

HOW TO RESPOND **SUMMARY**

1 The overall objective in any conversation might be to agree, to disagree, to agree on the difference – and to have an enjoyable and interesting discussion.

2 If you are in any doubt about what has been said, it is important to ask for clarification. Misunderstanding and arguing at cross purposes are a waste of time and energy.

3 Support goes beyond agreement. You can support a point that has been made from statistics, from your own experience, from a shared set of values and so on.

4 Anecdotes, examples and stories add liveliness and reality to the discussion. They may be stories from your own experience or ones you have heard and believe to be relevant.

5 Stories do not 'prove' anything except perhaps to challenge a generalisation (by showing exceptions).

6 Stories illustrate principles, processes and possibilities. A process that might be complex to explain can be illustrated by a simple story.

7 You may want to go further than just agreeing with a point that has been made. You may want to build upon that point in order to take it further.

8 You may wish to extend a suggestion by enlarging it and growing the suggestion.

9 You can imagine an idea being put into action in the real world. You watch what might happen and

     describe what you see: in both a positive and
     negative sense.

10   You may want to modify an idea to make it more
     acceptable to yourself, stronger or more practical.

11   Once an idea has emerged it is no longer a matter of
     'your idea' or 'my idea' but an idea to be improved
     and assessed.

12   Instead of the usual 'battle' of argument there is a
     joint effort to explore the subject.

6 🌱 how to **listen**

A good listener is very nearly as attractive as a good talker. You cannot have a beautiful mind if you do not know how to listen.

A good listener shows that he or she is paying attention to what is being said.
A good listener respects the speaker.
A good listener shows that he or she is genuinely interested in what he or she hears.
A good listener gets value from what is heard and shows that he or she is getting value.

All the above are to do with real attitudes and not just pretended attitudes. Unless you are going to be talking all the time, you are going to have to listen. So, do it well and get the most out of listening.

IMPATIENCE

There are few things uglier than a listener who does not want to listen and is only waiting for the moment that he or she can speak. This impatience is usually very visible and is offensive to the speaker.

If you do not want to listen to anyone else then why should anyone else want to listen to you?

You may feel that what you have to say is more important than what others have to say – but that is probably not a view shared by the others.

So listen carefully and attentively and you should get more value than if you are just impatiently waiting for a chance to do your own talking.

GETTING VALUE

If you listen carefully and attentively you will get more value from listening than from talking.

Talking can show how smart you are. Talking can convince others of your views. Talking can help you clarify your own thinking. But talking only rarely gives you something new. Listening, on the other hand, can give you new ideas – if you try to receive them.

There may be information that you did not know. You could, for example, find out why some countries drive on the right of the road and others on the left of the road.

There may be new facts. For example, statistics might be given. You may want to check these with a question before accepting them. Did you know that 95 per cent of US criminal cases are settled by plea bargaining? Did you know that in many countries more people are killed in road accidents through the driver falling asleep than through alcohol?

There may be a point of view you have not heard before. Smokers pay their pension contributions in the same way as everyone else. But smokers often live shorter lives (up to eight years shorter, depending on the extent of the smoking). So smokers often do not draw down the full pension to which they have contributed. So smokers are subsidising non-smokers – which is very altruistic of them.

There may be new insights and realisations. In the USA there are twenty-seven times as many lawyers per head of the population as in Japan. Law is one of the most popular faculties at universities. In Japan the total number of lawyers allowed to practise is itself limited by law. Why so many lawyers in the USA? Law is seen as a general-purpose qualification that both serves as a back-up and also allows you to do other things. It may also be that intelligent youngsters who want a mentally challenging profession but do not like mathematics go in for law. Law is one of the very few professions that do not demand a high expertise in mathematics as a gateway requirement.

You may gain new, alternative perceptions. You might always have looked at something in one way and, through listening, you find that there is another way of looking at the same thing. Perhaps you perceive retirement as a time for resting. The new perception is that, on the contrary, it is the time for even more activity – but doing things you have always wanted to do and not been able to do. You may have perceived some person's rudeness as aggression and then come to see it as a cover for insecurity.

You may find value in seeing how a point of view, totally different from your own, is put together rationally. You could listen to someone who genuinely believes that prolonging life at all costs is not a good use of resources. It is said that in the USA some 75 per cent of health care costs are spent in the last month of life. You might listen to 'pro-choice' and 'pro-life' views with regard to abortion.

You may find value in discovering what values matter to different people. What are these values? How do they operate these values?

Contrast someone sifting through mud to find diamonds and someone walking along a beach looking at the driftwood. The diamond seeker has to go through a lot of mud to find a single diamond. But the person knows what a diamond looks like and knows the market value (or sale value) of the diamond. This is equivalent to looking for things of known value.

However, the person walking along the beach looking at the driftwood is not looking for something of 'known value'. This person 'finds value' in the unusual shape of the driftwood, which might make a good lamp, or a walking stick.

So value may be defined and recognisable, or it may be what you bring to something that creates the value. Perhaps something already in your mind can be put together with something you hear in order to create a new value.

NOTICE

Take note of the words being used. Take note especially of the adjectives. Adjectives are almost always subjective. Adjectives tell you what the person feels rather than objective reality. (See also page 141.)

*That was a very boring journey. (In fact, the scenery was
    beautiful but the person had seen it all before.)*
*The restaurant was very exotic. (In fact, the restaurant was
    over-gaudy and rather vulgar – to someone else's eyes.)*
*He is arrogant and aloof. (In fact, the person is shy and
    reserved.)*

Pay attention to the turn of phrase and the analogies that are used. Some of them might be useful for you to use yourself in the future.

REPEAT BACK

This is a very useful part of listening. You repeat back to the speaker what you think that person has been saying.

Such repetition indicates that you have understood what was said. It also clarifies the situation in your own mind. For example:

I think I heard you say that recession is good for business in the long term because inefficient businesses are killed which leaves more market for the efficient businesses when the recession ends. Is that correct?

Are you saying that the USA may be the only industrialised country that really respects and admires success? Are you saying that in other countries, such as Britain, there is an automatic envy of success and attempts to bring it down?

Did I understand you to say that women might make better doctors than men because women are more intuitive and therefore likely to take many more factors into account?

Is it your point that increasing the punishment for crime is not really a deterrent if criminals feel that their chance of being caught is actually very small?

Are you saying that Korean immigrant groups do well because they have a powerful structure of 'self-help' groups through which they help each other?

To summarise, condense, recapitulate and feed back what has been understood is flattering to the speaker, who wants to know if his or her message has been received.

QUESTIONS

Questions are very much part of listening. They show attention and interest. They allow for the further exploration of certain points. They permit the clarification of any misunderstanding. They enable the speaker to elaborate on points which seem to be of interest to the listener. They can be used to check up on things. For instance:

Are those official figures or a ball-park guess?
Did Mr Horsley actually say that in your presence?
Did you see that with your own eyes or are you passing on
    what someone told you?
Is that a scientific fact?
Do the figures actually support the point you make about
    smokers?

Does that apply across all age groups or only youngsters (see the birthday explanation given previously)?

How many more accidents do these people have?

If the difference is only a few per cent it may be statistically significant but not have much practical value (like charging more for insurance).

If a speaker says, for example: 'In New Zealand it has been found that children from a severely dysfunctional family have an increased chance of becoming criminals,' this may not seem surprising. If you then ask what is the extent of the increased chance, you may well be surprised.

Such children seem to have one hundred times the likelihood of becoming criminals. That is a huge figure.

MORE DETAILS

You may ask for more details around a point which particularly interests you. For instance:

'Could you tell me more about these Korean self-help groups? How do they function?' This shows interest and attention and allows you to get far more value from your listening.

The speaker may be trying to make a point and has no way of knowing which part of his or her discourse is of most interest to his audience. It is up to the listeners to ask questions to get more details around the more interesting points. To take another example: 'China may be the only country in the world in which the suicide rate for women now exceeds the suicide rate for men.' Questions might be:

Is this a recent trend?
Is it related to the one child per family policy?
Is this across all age groups?
Is the figure the same for single and married women?

TWO FOCUSES

As you listen there are always at least two focuses.

The person speaking may be trying to make a point, to express an opinion or to create one side of an argument. You need to pay attention to this. What is the speaker trying to achieve? How well is the speaker achieving this? Do you agree with the speaker's main point? Is the speaker convincing?

Respect for the speaker means that you are listening to what the speaker is 'trying to do'.

At the same time there is a second focus.

Let us say you are driving along a road and you want to get to town 'B'. As you drive along you pass through a quaint village or you drive by an historic site. You stop to explore what has caught your interest.

So as you listen, the second focus is concerned with matters of interest that arise in what you hear but have little direct relevance to the case the speaker is trying to make. When you hear a reference to Korean self-help groups you want to know more about them because such social structures interest you.

If you hear that the prophet Muhammad in the Hadith (his own sayings) has several references to 'thinking', you may want to know what these references are.

The trick is to keep both focuses in mind if you are to get full value from listening. Suppose you only focus on the main argument being made. At the end you find you do not agree with the argument. If you have only focused on the argument you have gained very little. However, if you have also focused on the 'interest content' of what has been said, you may have learned important new information, alternative perceptions and different experiences (see also pages 49 and 163).

HOW TO LISTEN **SUMMARY**

1 The ability to listen and the enjoyment of listening is a key part of developing a beautiful mind.

2 A good listener pays attention and seeks to get the maximum value from what is being said. There are two focuses for attention: the point the speaker is trying to make; and the separate value of what is being said (in its own right).

3 Listening is not just having to wait impatiently until you can yourself speak.

4 You may get new information and you can probe for further information with questions.

5 You may get a new point of view which had not occurred to you before.

6 There may be new insights and realisations that are triggered by the speaker.

7 You might realise there are alternative perceptions that are new to you.

8 You may learn the reasoning behind a point of view quite different from your own.

9 You could learn how people apply values which differ from your own.

10 You should take note of the words used and especially the adjectives, which indicate feelings.

11 You should make a habit of repeating back to the speaker what you think you have understood. This is both useful and important.

12 You should use questions to check on facts and to ask for more details around points of interest.

7 🐝 questions

Questions are important because they are one of the main means of interaction between people in conversation or in any type of communication (see also page 72).

What would the world be like if we were not allowed to ask questions?

Ask this question to anyone you like. Most people would answer that life would be very difficult. It would be hard to communicate and almost impossible to get what we wanted if other people were involved.

The real answer is that it would make almost no difference at all.

A question is simply a way of directing attention. For example:

'What is your name?' This means: 'Direct attention to your name'; or even, 'Tell me your name.'

'Which country eats more chocolate per head than any other country?' This means: 'Direct attention to chocolate eating in different countries and tell me which one is at the top of the list.'

So we use questions to get someone to direct his or her attention to something we want or want to know.

The Greek philosopher Socrates had and has a great reputation for asking questions. But what sort of questions were they?

Socrates: If you were choosing your best athlete would you choose that person by chance? If you were choosing the best navigator for a ship, would you choose that person by chance?

Listener: Of course not.

Socrates: Why then do we choose our politicians by chance (in the last round)?

The listener is expected to say that chance is never the best way of getting the most able people.

The reason the Greeks did use chance was to avoid bribery, corruption and factions, which have nothing to do with athletics or navigation but everything to do with politics.

Socrates mainly asked 'leading questions'. Step by step the listener gave the 'expected answer' to a question and so had to reach the conclusion that Socrates wished the listener to reach.

Socrates rarely asked open-ended questions.

FISHING QUESTIONS AND SHOOTING QUESTIONS

In the CoRT programme (see page 6) a distinction is made between 'fishing questions' and 'shooting questions'.

A huntsman goes out with a gun. He shoots at a bird. There are only two possible outcomes: he hits the bird or he misses the bird (leaving out minor hits). There are two features here. We know what the man is aiming at. We know the range of possible outcomes.

In a 'shooting question', we know the target. We also know the range of possible outcomes – 'yes' or 'no'. For example:

Did you go shopping this morning?
Is George W. Bush the fortieth president of the USA?
You went to Cornell, did you not?

All these questions can be answered by a simple 'yes' or 'no'. That is what the questioner intends. A shooting question is always designed to be answered by a yes or no.

The main purpose of a shooting question is to check on something, where what is to be checked falls within a limited range.

If you wanted to know in which month someone's birthday fell you could ask: 'Is your birthday in January?' If you got the answer no you would then ask: 'Is your birthday in February?' And so on through all the months of the year until you got a yes.

It might be more efficient to ask: 'Does your birthday fall in the first six months of the year?' If the answer was yes, you would then ask: 'Is your birthday in the first three months of the year?' In this way the number of questions needed would be considerably reduced.

It would, of course, be much simpler to ask: 'In which month does your birthday fall?'

We now come to 'fishing questions'. When you go fishing you sit by the stream and cast your bait. You do not know exactly which fish you are going to catch or whether you will catch any fish at all. It is much more open-ended than shooting at a particular bird.

So, fishing questions are open-ended. The questioner does not know what answer will be given. For example:

What is the most popular girl's name in the USA?
Who won the 100 metres race at the Sydney Olympics?
What is the best treatment for sinusitis?

The range of answers is, however, limited by the nature of the question. The answer to the question about the most popular girl's name would not have been 'Cornflakes'.

The person asking the question may or may not know the answer, or may offer a guess (I think it is so). The answer may sometimes be 'none' but this is still different from a shooting question.

Fishing question: Who were the female presidents of the USA?
Answer: There have not been any female presidents.

Shooting question: Have there been any female presidents of the USA?
Answer: No.

If you suspected that the answer to your question might be 'no' you would ask a shooting question. If you had no idea you would ask a fishing question. 'How many father and son presidents of the USA have there been? And who were they?'

If you know exactly what you want to check on then a shooting question is appropriate. Otherwise a fishing question, at least at first, is more efficient. 'What is the date of the statistics you are quoting?' may be more effective than asking: 'Are those statistics recent?'

SOURCE AND VALIDITY

An obvious use of questions is to check on the source and validity of figures, stories, reports, for example. Is there an objective report which anyone can look at? If an argument rests on certain points then you do need to check the source of those points. You might say: 'Is that your direct personal experience or are you quoting someone else?'

There is a big difference between objective measurement and personal opinion. Even if you believe the data is from an official source, it is always worth checking with a question.

MORE DETAIL

Perhaps the most frequent use of questions is to ask for more detail, or elaboration around a point: 'Could you tell me more about that?'

You may need the elaboration in order to understand the matter more fully. You may need the elaboration purely out of interest.

When figures are given it could be important to know the relevant detail. How big was the sample? Was this a mixed age group? Do the figures hold across age and gender? How was the survey done? This is not so much to check the figures but more to extract more information from the figures.

EXPLANATION

'Is an explanation given for this?'

You can ask for an official explanation if one has been offered. You can ask the person offering the information for his or her explanation. You might then proceed to offer your own possible explanation.

Science is all about hypotheses, which are provisional explanations for perceived events.

Sometimes an explanation will have been investigated and proved correct. You need to know this.

ALTERNATIVES AND POSSIBILITIES

'What are the alternatives?'
'What are the possibilities?'

There are four levels of alternatives and possibilities:

1 *Alternatives and possibilities that have been officially considered and have been checked out.*

2 *Alternatives and possibilities that are official but have not yet been checked out.*

3 *Alternatives and possibilities which the speaker has generated but not checked out.*

4 *The additional alternatives and possibilities that you, as a listener, can suggest.*

The ability to generate possibilities enriches the discussion but also frees us from the certainty that something 'must be so' only because we cannot think of an alternative explanation. (See also page 44.)

The speaker may be asked: 'Would you accept this possibility?'

Some people have difficulty with possibilities on the basis that if everything is possible, how can any decision be reached? Yet the procedure is quite straightforward. In the 'consideration' phase you need to open up possibilities. In the 'action' phase you need to narrow down to probabilities and specific actions. You would not stand on the top of a burning building hoping that Batman might swoop down and rescue you.

MODIFICATION

A listener may have difficulty with an extreme position taken by a speaker. The listener may want to modify the proposition to make it more realistic and more acceptable. He or she might say: 'Would you accept this modification to your proposition?'

There may be certain core elements the speaker does not want to modify at all. For example, he or she may want police forces to be as ethnically balanced as the areas in which the force works. Does this mean that merit has to be put aside in order to get this balance? That can be asked directly as a question. There is also a modified position:

'All other things, including merit, being equal, then an effort should be made to get the ethnic balance. Would you accept this version?'

The speaker may not accept it on the basis that no effort will be made to improve education and skills if the modification is accepted.

Or, 'Has this alternative been considered?'

MULTIPLE CHOICE QUESTIONS

The listener may pose a question in which the speaker is asked to choose between a limited range of answers. Many speakers will object and claim that the answer lies outside the boxes, between the boxes or in more than one box. Nevertheless, it can be useful to try this sort of question from time to time:

'In your experience, are women in business a) more decisive than men; b) less decisive than men; c) no different at all from men?'

The answer might be that there is no general picture but a lot of individual variation.

Another multiple choice question might be: 'Would you say that heart disease was related to any one of these factors more than the others: a) genetics; b) race; c) life- style; d) diet?'

And another: 'Which of the following themes is mentioned most often by politicians in their election promises: a) health; b) education; c) taxation; d) employment; e) economic growth; f) crime?'

The answer is 'education' and almost every US president declares himself to be 'the education president'.

Would you say that it was economic factors or social factors which drove teenage crime?

VALUES

People do not like talking about values. It is assumed that they are obvious. It is assumed that everyone shares the same basic values – freedom, for example. Values are private and talking about values is somewhat like talking about sex.

You may not get an answer but it is possible to ask what values are in use when a proposition is put forward: 'In your views on prison and punishment what are your key values?'

Values put forward might include: justice; protection of society; deterrence; restitution; rehabilitation of criminals; cost to society. The next question might ask about the hierarchy – Which values come first? Which are the dominant values?

Questions about values can be put as multiple choice questions: 'In times of heightened sensitivity regarding terrorism, which value should come first: protection of innocent people in society or individual human rights?' Or: 'Which is more important, the greater good or individual moral principles (is it permissible to tell a lie if this results in a greater good?)?'

THE BASIS FOR YOUR THINKING?

This is a key question. Someone is putting forward a proposition. The listener listens and understands what is being said. Then the listener asks: 'What is the basis for your thinking (your feelings, your decision, your proposal)?'

The speaker may feel that he or she has already made the basis clear. The speaker may also reply in generalities: a) clear reason; b) personal experience; c) pragmatism; d) the need to do something; e) sense of outrage; f) compassion; g) human values.

Through further questions the listener may seek to get the speaker to be more explicit: Outrage about what? Compassion for whom? What personal experience? Why is there a need to do something?

QUESTIONS **SUMMARY**

1   Questions are a key means of interaction in any conversation or discussion. A listener should seek to ask questions.

2   A question is a way of 'directing attention' to some matter. A question is a polite way of demanding something.

3   With a 'shooting question', you know that the answer you will get is a 'yes' or a 'no'. Such question are used to check things out.

4   A 'fishing question' is more open-ended. You do not know what answer you will get except that it will be related to the question.

5   A person asked a question may give the answer, not know the answer, guess or challenge the question.

6   Questions are essential to challenge the validity and source of information that is being used to support an argument.

7   Questions are also vital to ask for more detail and elaboration around a point.

8   You can ask for explanations whether official or personal.

9   You can request alternatives and possibilities and confirm that your own suggestions make sense.

10   You can check if your modification of an offered position is acceptable.

11   You can frame a question as a multiple-choice question.

12   You can ask for the values in use and also the underlying basis of what is being proposed. What is the basis for your thinking?

8 ✿ parallel thinking –
the six hats

For about two thousand four hundred years we have been satisfied with argument as a way of thinking. The method was designed by the Greek Gang of Three: Socrates, Plato and Aristotle.

Argument is an excellent method and has served us well. At the same time, as we have seen, it is unsophisticated. Each side makes a 'case' and then seeks to defend that case and prove the other 'case' to be wrong. It says, in short: 'I am right and you are wrong.' (See also Chapter 5.)

In argument the motivation may be high because it is an aggressive motivation. The actual exploration of the subject is low. As mentioned in Chapter 2, a prosecutor in a court of law will not mention points which help the defence case and will certainly not make an effort to find them. The same holds for the defence attorney.

We use argument not because we think it is such a wonderful method – but because we do not know any other method.

In 1985 I designed the alternative method of 'parallel thinking', which is now widely used in business and in education: from four-year-olds in school to senior executives in some of the world's largest corporations. One corporation used to spend thirty days on their multi-national project discussions. Using parallel thinking, they do the same thing in two days. Wage negotiations in a mine used to take three weeks. Using parallel thinking, they are now concluded in forty-five minutes. On another occasion a union said to management that they refused to negotiate unless the method of parallel thinking was used. MDS, a company in Canada, reckoned they saved $20 million in the first year they used parallel thinking. Siemens, the largest corporation in Europe, estimated they reduced product development time by 50 per cent using the method. Some judges in the USA are having their juries use the method – with very promising results.

The method is widely used in family discussions because it allows every party to put forward their thinking.

Parallel thinking is very different from the 'ego-driven' and 'battle-oriented' method of argument. Those who have got used to the method find a return to argument very primitive.

In one school the staff used the method in their own discussions as well as teaching the method to the pupils. One day there were visitors who did not know the method, so the staff went back to normal argument, and reported that argument now seemed crude and unsatisfactory.

CO-OPERATIVE EXPLORATION

Imagine there are four people standing around a square building. Each person is facing a different side. Each person insists that what he or she sees is the proper view of the building. They argue via walkie-talkies.

In parallel thinking each person would walk round to one side of the building. They would now each describe what they saw. Then they would all walk around to another side of the building and again describe what they saw. The same procedure for the third side, and then the fourth side.

So, all parties look at the matter from the same point of view and describe what they see. In the end there has been a full exploration of the building (the matter being discussed).

For the method of work, it is essential that at any moment everyone is looking 'in parallel' in the same direction.

THE SIX THINKING HATS

In 1985 I devised the Six Hats method of better thinking, a method that will help you enhance your conversation and so develop a beautiful mind.

The metaphor of six coloured hats – white, red, black, yellow, green and blue – is used to align the thinkers or members of the discussion so that they are all looking in the same direction at any one time. It is essential that everyone is wearing the same hat at the same moment. It is completely wrong for different people to be wearing different hats.

Why hats?

You can put on or take off a hat easily and deliberately.

Hats have an association with thinking – 'Put on your thinking cap.'

Hats are used to indicate roles – 'Wearing my police hat/my parent hat' and so on.

There is no need for there to be physical hats. Many boardrooms around the world now have posters of the hats on the wall or small symbolic hats that can be put on the table. The hats are, nevertheless, metaphorical.

THE WHITE HAT

The white hat suggests paper and computer print-outs. The white hat means 'information'. When the white hat is in use everyone is focusing on information.

It is no longer the usual matter of one person saying something and another person disagreeing. When the white hat is in use, everyone is focusing on information – in parallel.

What do we know?
What do we need to know?
What is missing?

What questions should we ask?
How might we get the information we need?

Information can range from hard facts, which can be checked, to soft information like rumours and personal experience.

If the information conflicts then both versions are put down alongside each other. For example:

'The last plane for New York leaves at 9.30 pm', and 'The last plane for New York leaves at 10.30 pm.' Both versions are noted. When it becomes important to check which may be true, then at that point the effort is made to see which version is right.

Every person involved is now making a full effort to explore the subject and to lay out the information available and the information needed. It is no longer a matter of only looking for the information that fits your point of view and your case.

It is not unlike asking everybody 'to look north' and to report what they see. Each person now makes an effort to describe what he or she sees as accurately as possible.

THE RED HAT

Think of red as fire and warm. The red hat represents emotions, feelings and intuition.

This is a very important hat. In normal thinking your feelings and emotions are not supposed to come in. Of course, the emotions do come in – you merely disguise them as logic. So if emotions are not allowed they influence all the thinking offered.

The red hat allows emotions and feeling. The red hat legitimises emotions and gives them a formal place:

I do not like this idea at all.
My feeling is that this simply will not work.
My intuition is that raising the price will destroy the market.
My gut feeling is that this is highly dangerous.
I feel it is a waste of time.

A very important point is that under the red hat you do not have to give any reasons at all for your 'feelings'. You just express your feelings. They exist in you – so you express them. The reason for this is that in many cases the reasons behind the feelings are not clearly known (as in intuition) and therefore people would not put forward their feelings if they could not give reasons, so no reasons should be given – even if the reasons are known.

Intuition can be based on experience in the field. For instance:

My intuition is that she is the right person for the job.
My intuition is that the costs on this project will escalate rapidly.
My intuition is that there are internal office politics behind that decision.
My intuition is that the economy will start to turn up in the next quarter.

Intuition is a complex judgement. The thinker may not even be aware of all the components that go into the judgement. Intuition is often right – but not always. When they told the great Einstein about Heisenberg's Uncertainty Principle, Einstein replied that his intuition was that nature did not work that way and that 'God did not play dice'. It seems Einstein's intuition was wrong. In the end intuition can only be based on personal experience and personal thinking.

Nevertheless, intuition is a useful ingredient, a useful component, in thinking. There are some areas where decisions have to be made on intuition because there is no other way: 'My intuition is that this proposal will not be acceptable to both sides and the conflict will continue.' Or: 'My intuition is that this fashion will not catch on.'

When there is no other way of checking something then intuition plays an important role. At other times intuition is an ingredient or one factor to be taken into account.

THE BLACK HAT

This is the most used of hats in normal behaviour. The black hat is the basis of 'critical thinking'. The word 'critical' comes from the Greek 'kritikos', which means judge, and critical thinking is judgement thinking: is this right or is it wrong? The basis of argument and western thinking in general is the black hat.

The black hat is an excellent hat and probably the most useful of all the hats. The black hat stops us from doing things that are wrong, illegal or dangerous.

I prefer to use the word 'caution' with the black hat. Other words might be 'careful' or 'risk assessment' and we can ask ourselves: 'Does this fit?'

Does this fit our values?
Does this fit our resources?
Does this fit our strategy and objectives?
Does this fit our abilities?

Because the black hat may point out dangers, faults and problems, it does not make it a 'bad hat'. A doctor who deals with illness is not therefore a bad person. The look-out on a ship who indicates that there are reefs ahead is an excellent person.

The black hat can be used in a number of different ways:

to indicate a fault in logic (that does not follow . . .)
to point out incorrect information
to point out faults and weaknesses
to point out why something does not fit
to point out the 'downside'
to point out potential problems

In general the black hat covers all 'caution' aspects.

THE YELLOW HAT

The black hat is very much part of our thinking culture in argument and elsewhere. It is also very much part of education. Since the purpose of education is to tell youngsters 'how the world really is' there is a need to let them know when they have got something wrong.

In contrast, the yellow hat is almost entirely neglected. Under the yellow hat we look for values, benefits and why something *should* work.

This positive aspect of thinking is largely neglected.

We need to develop 'value sensitivity'. This means being sensitive to value. Without value sensitivity, creativity can be a waste of time. I have sat in on creative meetings where good ideas were generated, but even the people generating the ideas could not see the full value of their own ideas.

Value sensitivity means looking at something with the intention of finding the values in it. We are very ready to find fault – but not at all ready to find value. The bias is entirely towards the negative.

Under the yellow hat major insights can happen. People suddenly see values they have never seen before. There can be sudden revelations about values which are not very obvious.

The yellow hat invites everyone to make an effort to find value.

Suppose someone is very much against an idea which has been proposed. Under the black hat that person points out all the dangers and disadvantages of the idea. Then it is the turn of the yellow hat and everyone is supposed to find values. If that person cannot see any value in the idea but everyone else can, then that person is seen to be stupid. If everyone can see value, why can you not see value? This is very different from argument, where you make no effort at all to find value in an idea you do not like. Under the yellow hat every thinker is 'challenged' to find value.

In argument you show off by winning arguments, by attacking the other point of view and defending your own. With parallel thinking you show off by performing better under every hat. So under the black hat you think of more caution points than anyone else, and under the yellow hat you think of more value points than anyone else. In this way all the brain power available is seeking to explore the subject honestly and thoroughly. It is no longer a matter of making a case or winning an argument. In practice, the difference between the two approaches is huge.

Would you buy an expensive car and then put inferior gas into the tank?

Why pay good brains a high salary and then only get part of their thinking? Because parallel thinking encourages every thinker to think 'fully and objectively' about a subject, the method is becoming increasingly used in business.

Imagine a boardroom meeting with several very clever and experienced people sitting around the table. Someone is talking and proposing a strategy. What is everyone else doing? Mostly they are trying to find a fault in what is said. This allows them to contribute and to exercise their ego. What a huge waste of brain power that it should be limited to operating only in the critical mode!

Why pay high salaries to clever people and then choose to use only part of their thinking?

THE GREEN HAT

Think of vegetation, growth and energy. Think of branches and sprouting. Think of creative energy.

The green hat is the productive hat. The green hat is the generative hat. The green hat is the creative hat.

The black and yellow hats are judgement hats. The white hat asks for information. The red hat asks for feelings, emotions and intuition.

The green hat asks for ideas, alternatives, possibilities and designs.

What can we do? What are the alternatives?

Why did this happen? What are the possible explanations? The chairman might say: 'We need some new ideas here.' Or: 'Let's have both the obvious alternatives and some new ones.' Or: 'We need some green hat thinking right here.'

The green hat is an invitation to creativity.

Instead of creativity happening when one person has an idea and everyone else gets ready to jump on that idea and attack it, creativity is now a formal request. Under the green hat there is a time, place and expectation for creative thinking. Everyone is challenged and 'put on the spot'. You are required to make a creative effort and a creative contribution. If not you keep quiet.

What is especially interesting, in practice, is that people who have never considered themselves to be creative suddenly make a creative effort and find that they are much more creative than they had thought themselves to be. People who would never have interjected a creative idea into a serious meeting now find that when creativity is an 'expectation' they can produce new ideas.

These may be ideas that are in use elsewhere. They may be new ideas that a person has had for some time. They may be new ideas that are produced there and then through natural creativity. They may be new ideas produced through the formal and deliberate use of lateral thinking tools such as provocation and random entry, for instance.

The search for alternatives should always include the obvious ones. This is followed by a search for less obvious alternatives and an attempt to generate new alternatives. Simple and almost obvious ideas can be as useful as exotic ideas.

New ideas can range from ideas which are very logical once they have been expressed through ideas that are probable to ones that are just possible and, finally, to ideas that are on the side of fantasy (but which can still serve to provoke good ideas).

Once the habit of creativity has been established with the green hat, it is surprising how productive it can be.

THE BLUE HAT

Think 'blue sky' and overview. The blue hat is like the conductor of the orchestra. The role of the blue hat is to organise the other hats and to organise the thinking.

The blue hat is to do with process control.

At the beginning of the discussion the blue hat has two main functions. The first of these is defining the focus and purpose.

What are we here for? What are we thinking about? What is the end goal?

The blue hat at the beginning defines the focus. There may be a consideration of alternative focuses or even sub-focuses. Everyone can take part in this discussion with suggestions and opinions. In the end the chairman of the session makes the decision.

The blue hat's second function at the beginning is to lay out the sequence of hats for the session. Again this can be a matter for discussion.

What sequence of hats are we going to use?

During the discussion itself the blue hat has largely a control function. For example:

We are in the yellow hat right now, your remark is rather black hat.'
Under the red hat you just express your feelings, you do not give the reasons behind the feelings.
This is green hat time. We need some new ideas.

The blue hat can also adjust the sequence of hats that has been pre-set. For example, if the red hat shows that most people dislike the idea then the black hat can be placed next to allow people to explain their dislike. So small changes in the sequence are made under the blue hat.

At the end the blue hat has an important function. The blue hat puts together the outcome, the summary, the conclusion and the design. What have we achieved?

If nothing has been achieved then the reason for this can be put forward: 'We need more information in this area.' Or: 'There is a lack of suggestions as to ways out of this mess.'

The blue hat also lays out the next step at the end. This next step could take the form of more thinking or of action. If additional information is needed then ways of getting this new information are decided upon.

The blue hat at the beginning and the blue hat at the end are like two bookends that bracket the thinking. What are we here for? What have we achieved?

Although the blue hat welcomes discussion and suggestions, the final decision is made by the chairman, facilitator or leader of the group.

USE OF THE HATS

The hats provide a strong and neutral symbol of requesting a type of thinking.

'That's great black hat thinking, now let's have some yellow hat on this.'

'Give me your red hat.'

'What is the white hat here?'

Such requests could indeed be expressed in ordinary language but the artificiality of the six hats provides a stronger code.

'Some green hat, please' is stronger than just asking for more creative thinking.

'What is your red hat here?' is more powerful than asking someone to express their feelings – which they are not used to doing.

So the hats can be used individually as a code requesting a specific type of thinking.

The hats can also be used as a pre-set sequence for exploring a subject. The sequence will vary according to the purpose of the thinking: exploration; problem solving; creative thinking; conflict resolution; design. For each of these situations the sequence will vary.

In ordinary conversation the hats are mainly used individually. For those who want full training in the use of the hats for organisational and business purposes, this can be arranged (see www.aptt.com or fax UK +44 (0) 207602 1779).

BENEFITS

The hats provide an alternative to argument. The hats allow joint exploration of a subject. The hats require each individual fully to explore a subject rather than just to make and defend a case. The hats provide a quick method of switching thinking. The hats provide a means to request a particular type of thinking. The hats replace the ego and aggression of argument with the challenge thoroughly to explore a subject. The hats get the best out of people.

Meeting times can be reduced to one fifth or even less, using the hats. The hats are easy to learn and to use. The hats are in use with four-year-olds and with senior executives. It is no longer necessary to use argument simply because there is no other method of discussion.

PARALLEL THINKING – THE SIX HATS
SUMMARY

1   In traditional argument each side prepares a case
    and then seeks to defend that case and to attack the
    other case. Actual exploration of the subject is
    limited.

2   Parallel thinking replaces the battle of argument
    with a joint exploration of the subject as all parties
    think 'in parallel' at any moment.

3   The direction of thinking is indicated by six coloured
    hats, each of which indicates a mode of thinking. At
    any moment everyone is 'wearing' the same colour of
    hat. That is what is meant by 'parallel thinking'.

4   The white hat indicates a focus on information.
    What do we have? What do we need? How are we
    going to get the information we need?

5   The red hat gives full permission for the expression
    of feelings, emotions and intuition without any need
    to give the reasons behind the feelings.

6   The black hat is for 'caution' and the focus is on
    faults, weaknesses, what might go wrong and why
    something does not 'fit'.

7   With the yellow hat the focus is on values, benefits
    and how something can be done.

8   The green hat sets aside time, space and expectation
    for creative effort. Under the green hat everyone is
    expected to make such an effort.

9 The blue hat is to do with the organisation of thinking. This means setting up the focus and also putting together the outcome.

10 The hats can be used as single hats to request a specific type of thinking. This allows a rapid change in thinking.

11 The hats can also be used as a pre-set sequence to explore a subject. The sequence will vary with the type of thinking needed.

12 The hats make sure that everyone is using his or her thinking fully to explore the subject. If you want to show off you now do this by out-performing others on each hat.

9 🌴 concepts

Concepts are a very important part of thinking. If you want to have a beautiful mind you need to be able to handle concepts. However, most people find 'concepts' vague, abstract and academic. This is especially so in the USA where there is a hunger for practical, hands-on, do-it-now instructions.

Concepts are the parents of practical ideas. If you can locate the parents of a child then you can find the brothers and sisters and even other relatives of that child.

Once upon a time the mayor of a small town in Australia told me that they had a problem with commuters who drove into the town in the morning and left their cars parked in the street all day. This meant that shoppers could not find anywhere to park in order to visit the shops.

What is the operating 'concept' of a parking meter? The concept could be 'to get revenue from people's need to park'. That may happen but is probably not the main purpose. Another concept might be 'to get as many people as possible to use the same parking space in a day'. This seems more likely.

Now if that is the concept then we can 'carry out' that concept in another way: No parking meters (save capital costs) and you can park anywhere you like in marked spaces. But – you have to leave your headlights full on!

You would not want to leave your car parked for more than a few minutes as you would be running your battery down. So people would park, run into the shop and hurry back as quickly as possible. Of course, there are a lot of practical flaws in this idea, such as forgetful people, but it could be implemented in certain defined areas.

> *You always eat 'food'. But do you ever actually eat 'food' as such? You do not. You eat steak, you eat chicken, you eat strawberries. You always eat some specific type of food and not 'food' in general. Food is a concept. A hamburger is the practical idea.*

WHY BOTHER WITH CONCEPTS?

One of the main values of identifying a concept is that this allows us to 'breed' other ideas from the concept. Maybe there are other ways of 'getting maximum usage of limited parking space'.

Most attempts to deal with traffic congestion in cities have one major flaw. If traffic is reduced through people leaving their cars at home, those who benefit most are those who do not leave their cars at home – and now have clearer streets.

So we set up a 'concept objective'. How do we reward those who do leave their cars at home?

One approach is to require everyone who wants to drive into the city to buy a special permit, which would be displayed. Every car owner is entitled to buy one such permit. To drive into the city, however, you actually need three permits. So what do you do? You buy the two additional permits from someone who leaves his or her car at home. That person now 'gets paid' for not driving into the city. If there is a scarcity of permits then the price goes up and only those willing to pay the higher price can drive into the city. The operating concept is to 'put a price on driving into the city'.

The concept of 'putting a price on driving into the city' could be carried out in another way with a simple auction of a limited number of permits. This last idea, however, does not reward those who leave their cars at home.

PICK OUT THE CONCEPT

Let us take the following example: What is the concept of accident insurance?

The concept might be that all those exposed to the risk contribute to those who actually suffer from the accident.

In another example, domestic dogs and cats and rabbits come under the concept of 'pets'. That could also include canaries and white mice. How would you define the concept of a pet?

You might suggest that it is 'a living creature kept at home for no practical purpose other than to be loved'.

This is not completely correct because your cat might catch mice and your dog may act as a watch dog. So we might amend the concept: 'a living creature kept at home for the main purpose of being loved (including companionship)'.

Whenever you are listening to someone talking you should be making an effort to pick out the concept used. This is a sort of shorthand, a summary, the underlying essence of what is being said.

Take a discussion on education in which changes in education are suggested. You think you have picked out the suggested concept change as follows:

'The old concept of education was to develop a liberal mind that was cultured and could then learn to do anything. A lot of subject matter was taught to develop this "mind". The new concept might be to equip youngsters to function in society and to contribute to society. This means much more emphasis on thinking skills, learning how value is created in society, practical mathematics and so on. Is that correct?'

There are words which do seem to describe these two concepts: 'liberal education' and 'utilitarian education'. Unfortunately, the word 'utilitarian' has a restricted negative meaning. It suggests that you educate people immediately as carpenters, plumbers and shop assistants, for instance. This is quite different from teaching thinking skills or value creation in society. It often happens that if concept words do exist then we risk being forced to look at things in these standard ways. In fact, the type of education suggested falls between the existing concepts of 'liberal education' and 'utilitarian education'.

The same thing happens with the direct teaching of thinking. Educators say: 'Philosophy does that.' This is not true at all. Philosophy does not teach the practical operations of thinking. Even when philosophy does teach 'logic', this is only a small part of everyday thinking, where perception is even more important than logic.

When you believe you have extracted the concept from what is being said, you can check on this by asking a question: 'It seems to me that the concept here is . . . Is that correct?'

VAGUENESS

Concepts always seem rather vague. You can imagine a hamburger. You can see a hamburger. You can taste a hamburger. You can enjoy a hamburger. You cannot do these things with the vague concept of 'food'. You can go to the pet shop to buy a puppy or a kitten. You cannot go with the vague idea of buying 'a pet'.

In daily life you can probably get by very well without ever thinking of 'concepts'. But if you want to generate new ideas, design ways forward or understand complex situations, then you need to develop some skill with concepts.

The word 'reward' is a concept. The reward may take various forms: a smile; a star given by a teacher; monetary reward; a prize; recognition; promotion. A reward is an appreciation of effort and achievement. The concept is vague but very useful and very practical.

Say an employer wants to reward his staff. The concept comes first and then he or she needs to figure out how to do it and what sort of reward would mean most to the staff.

You set off on a journey. You know the roads that you need to take. You do not consciously say, 'Now I am heading north.' You take the road you know and happen to be heading north.

If, however, you are setting out on a long journey and are not familiar with the roads, then the instructions might be, 'Head north until you come to Castleford and then head due east until you reach Terence.' Here, the broad directions are very important. It is exactly the same with concepts.

When you are dealing with things with which you are familiar you do not seem to need concepts (even though they are there). When you are dealing with less familiar matters, then concepts become very useful.

'Don't tell me to buy "food". Tell me exactly what you want me to buy!'

You do not go out into the street in your underwear, although usually you are wearing underwear. The underwear is not visible but is there all the time. It is the same with concepts. They are there. They underlie the practical things we do – even when we are not conscious of them.

LEVELS OF CONCEPT

This is yet another difficulty when dealing with concepts. What level of concept do we use?

'Food' is a concept. But so is 'protein'. You could even say 'steak' was a concept because there are many different types of steak. So we have three levels of concept from the very broad to the more specific. How do you know which level to use?

There is no magic rule for choosing the level of concept to use.

Sometimes the very broad level is appropriate. An aid agency might say: 'People need food and shelter.' That might suggest that any sort of food would do. In the Irish potato famine (caused by a blight on potato crops), the British government sent over wheat, which was useless because the Irish did not know how to use, cook or eat the wheat.

On the whole, very broad concepts are not much use – except to contrast different concepts, such as: 'Should we run education on the basis of "reward" or on the basis of "punishment"?' Here, the very broad concepts do serve a purpose.

At the other extreme are concepts that are so specific they are almost practical ideas. While 'steak' is a concept it excludes fish, chicken and pasta. The danger with concepts that are too specific is that they narrow the thinking.

If you think only in terms of the concept of 'monetary reward' rather than 'reward' you may not realise that a smile, a word of appreciation or some sort of recognition might mean more to your staff than money.

'Achievement' is a broad concept. Youngsters need achievement. If we narrowed that concept to 'success in sports' then we might build more sports facilities. But there are many youngsters who are not interested in sport. There may also be much cheaper ways of providing achievement.

The general rule for concepts is: not too broad and not too specific. In practice, you would try out different levels of concept to find the level that seemed to work best. You come to get a 'feel' for the right level.

TYPES OF CONCEPT

Just as there are different levels of concept, there can be different types of concept.

Someone comes up with a new business idea. This is to create 'fast food' with no premises. So a central kitchen produces 'Pete's Food'. This is food of a standard type, quality and price. Any eating place can have a notice in the window saying: 'We also serve Pete's Food at Pete's Prices.' What are the concepts involved here?

There are the *business concepts*. No need to have your own expensive real estate: you use other people's places. Because the range is limited and the product is standard there is less wastage and more economy of scale. Instead of having many kitchens you have one central kitchen. Then there is the concept of 'branding'. You can put money into advertising the brand in a way no individual restaurant could afford to. The brand is also widely available so customers can develop brand loyalty.

Then there are the *customer value concepts*. There is the reassurance of the major brand name. This means quality and predictability: you know what you are getting regardless of the actual outlet. There is reassurance on price: you know what it will cost you. In fact, there are almost all the values available with traditional fast food chains. The ambience may not be guaranteed although even this could be remedied with inspection and standards so that unsuitable places did not get Pete's Food.

There is the *delivery concept.* This is a key part of business because without 'delivery' an idea is useless no matter how great it might be. The delivery concept is to make use of other people's premises. Delivery to these premises might be on a daily basis, or less often if the product can be stored.

> *There may be business concepts: why would this be a profitable business? There are mechanism or delivery concepts: how does this actually get done? There are value concepts: what are the real and perceived values to the buyer, client or customer? There are information concepts: how do people find out about this? There are acceptance concepts: why should people accept this idea? There are competition concepts: what might competitors do and how will this affect us?*

In short, there can be different types of concept. Every area can have its concepts just as every area can have its practical ideas.

EXERCISE

Concepts are tricky. Getting the concept habit is not easy. But instead of backing away from this most important component of the beautiful mind, it is worth putting some effort into developing the concept habit. Here is an exercise that will help develop just such a habit.

Make an effort to pick out the concept or concepts in each of the following situations. Do this on your own or compare, and discuss, your thinking with someone else (or a group). You should always try to pick out the major operating concept. You can also try to pick out the different types of concept in each case:

hotels
holidays
Internet
shoes
telephone
stairs
advertising
banks
bars
lawyers

COMPLETENESS

Concepts are rarely complete. Concepts capture the main 'essence' but may not cover all aspects.

What is the concept of a tree?

A way of centralising energy reception (from the sun) and water and nutrients (from the soil).

A way of putting together a volume of photosensitive material (leaves) in a more efficient way than spread out on the ground (grass).

A way of raising photosensitive material above the ground in a competitive environment (bushes and other trees block the sunlight).

A biological organism with long-term viability. Some trees live for eight hundred years. (Compare to the life of grass.)

Each of these is a valid concept. Not one covers the whole situation completely. There is instead a collection of relevant concepts. You could seek to put them all together in a single concept but it would be likely to be complex and far from complete.

Though they do overlap, a concept is not exactly the same as a definition. The definition of a Dalmatian may be 'a dog with a coat of black spots on a white background'. Of course, there is far more to a Dalmatian as any breeder would tell you. In fact, Dalmatians produce a special chemical in their urine which other dogs do not. The concept of a Dalmatian might be 'a striking-looking dog that is friendly and easy to train'.

The definition of an election might be 'the expression of choice by a group of people'. The concept might be 'a mechanism whereby those with a right to choose express their choice in an objective manner – and a readiness to accept the result of that choice'. The 'readiness to accept' might seem unnecessary but is in fact a key component.

COMPARE AND CONTRAST

Once you are comfortable dealing with concepts and extracting concepts from what is being said (or written) you can start to compare and contrast concepts.

How different is this concept from that one? Are these two apparently different concepts actually similar, and just expressions of one broader concept? Has the concept really changed or is this just a variation? Does this concept actually include the other concept (at a different level)? Working with concepts provides a different perspective and perception.

What is the concept of 'public transport'? Is the 'public' part important? Does this imply the concept of 'use without having to own'? Is a key component of public transport the fact that many people are moving in a comparatively small travelling space? This is high-density travel. If everyone in a bus had to get out and drive his or her own car, that would take up a great deal more space.

Is the concept 'pay for use only as required'? You do not have to own the bus, garage it or maintain it. Transport is now purchasable in small quantities.

There are negative concepts, too. Public transport is not available on demand both as to time and to starting point. There is limited flexibility with regard to choice of destination. There is less privacy.

CONCEPTS **SUMMARY**

1 Concepts are a very important part of thinking and a key component of a beautiful mind.

2 Concepts are like parents that breed children (ideas) and like road junctions that open up several other roads.

3 Concepts are important in generating ideas and designing ways forward. Where there is no routine available, concepts are essential.

4 You need to seek to pick out the concept behind what is being said (or read). What is the concept here?

5 Once you can pick out concepts you can compare and contrast them. Are they really different? What are the points of difference?

6 Concepts will always seem vague because they have to be translated into specific ideas before they can be used.

7 You can be using a concept without being aware of the concept you are using.

8 There may be different types of concept: business concept; value concept; mechanism concept; operating concept, etc. Wherever there are ideas there also are concepts.

9 There are different levels of concept from the very broad to the quite specific. In general, the middle layer is the most useful.

10 Concepts are not always complete but they carry important aspects of what is being thought or done.

11 Concepts, definitions and descriptions do overlap. Descriptions need to be complete, to define and separate. Concepts seek to distil the essence.

12 Skill in thinking in concept terms only comes with practice. Part of your mind should be watching and noticing the concepts being used by yourself and by others.

10 🌴 alternatives

Alternatives are so important a part of having a beautiful mind that they deserve a chapter on their own even though they have been mentioned in previous chapters (see pages 44 and 83). It could almost be said that the measure of the beauty of a mind is the ability of that mind to generate alternatives.

Why are alternatives so very important?

Alternatives are the opposite of rigidity. Being unwilling to look for alternatives indicates a very rigid mind that does not seek a better view of the world or a better way of doing things. It is a rigidity based on arrogance and defensiveness.

Alternatives are the opposite of complacency. If you are happy where you are and cannot imagine any improvement then you make no effort to find alternatives – or even to listen to them. Progress, energy, change, improvement and simplification are all based on the search for alternatives.

You know a problem is there and you want to get rid of it. So a lot of attention goes to problem solving and people spend a lot of time on problem solving.

But what if there is no problem? What if you do not have a stone in your shoe? What if you do not have a headache? Is there any need for thinking?

In a sense, having an adequate way of doing something is as much of a problem as a traditional problem. Is this adequate way the best? Should we be blocked from further thinking because we already have a way of doing something (or looking at something)?

BETTER

Imagine a television game for youngsters. On the floor are scattered some eggs. They are scattered about twenty feet from a red line. The boys work in pairs as a team. The task is to get all the eggs behind the red line – without breaking any. The winning team is the one that completes the task in the shortest possible time.

In one team, each boy goes out, picks up one or two eggs and carries them back over the red line. Both boys scurry back and forth, trying to be as fast as possible.

In another team, one boy stands behind the red line and the other boy stands amongst the eggs. The boy by the eggs picks them up one by one and tosses them to the other boy, who catches them and places them behind the red line. One or two eggs drop and get broken.

In another team, one boy takes off his shirt. The shirt is laid on the ground by the eggs and both boys load eggs on to the shirt. Each boy then takes hold of one end of the shirt and, carrying it like a hammock, they transport the eggs to the red line.

In yet another team, both boys take off their shirts. Each boy loads eggs on to his shirt on the ground. Each boy then drags his shirt, with the eggs lying on it, to the red line.

These are all alternative ways of carrying out the task. The winning team is the last team.

In this particular situation there is no fixed, usual or routine method so there is a challenge to find one, and as speed is the given value here any approach that increased speed is a 'better' approach.

In this example, making an effort to find a 'better' alternative paid off. How does this relate to real life?

The first point of difference is that in most real-life situations (other than problems) there is already a known method of doing things. It is not a matter of 'finding' a way as in the competition. If you have to find a way then you are inclined to look for alternatives. If you already have a way of proceeding, why should you look for a better way? You only do so if you realise the value of alternatives and are motivated to look for them.

In the competition, 'speed' was the measure of 'better'. In real life it is rare for there to be just one measure of 'better'. Doing something in a better way may involve many values. There is cost. There is speed. There is safety.

There is re-training. There is the disruption of change. There is resistance to change. All these are values and factors to be considered.

The main point is that having a way of doing something does not mean it is the best way of doing it.

Many years ago, in a seminar for the Post Office in the UK, I suggested that there was no need to put a value on stamps. The stamp would just carry an indicator of 'first class', etc. When you bought stamps you paid the prevailing price for the stamps. The stamps never changed. Some time later the Post Office did just this. I cannot prove a connection and that it was my idea which triggered the change, but it is a fact that I did suggest this idea. The change was away from decades of the traditional way of doing things.

In 1971 I ran a workshop for Shell Oil, in London. I suggested that instead of drilling oil wells in the traditional manner there might be an alternative way. The well would descend vertically to the level of the oil-bearing stratum and then would move horizontally along the stratum. Today, almost every oil well in the world is drilled this way. Why? Because this new way of drilling gives between three and six times as much oil per well. Again this was an 'alternative' to the very established traditional method of drilling for oil. I cannot prove that it was my workshop which triggered this idea. Others may have been working on the idea independently. Nevertheless, the alternative was given ahead of the use of the idea (from whatever source).

In both the above examples there was a sharp change from the traditional way of doing things.

There are really three stages:

1 *The willingness to set out to look for alternatives even in the most traditional situations. Because something has been done for a long time does not mean it is the best way. (Democracy is a classic example.)*

2 *The creative effort to generate alternatives. More than one alternative might be generated. This will depend on creative skill and the use of formal processes like lateral thinking (see page 48).*

3 *The assessment of the alternatives. The first level of assessment is to see if the alternative will really work and is acceptable. The second level of assessment is to determine what benefits the alternative offers and whether the benefits are sufficient to compensate for the cost of change. The third level of assessment is to choose amongst the different alternatives that have been generated.*

Many people feel that the whole process is too open-ended. You might put in a lot of effort and get no better alternatives. Many people feel the process demands a lot of thinking and are not willing to provide that. Then there is the risk factor: suppose the alternative turns out to be worse in practice?

So most people prefer not to look for alternatives. You can be blamed for not solving a problem but you cannot be blamed for not finding a better way of doing something.

In ordinary conversation, there are none of these risks. You can suggest possible alternatives knowing that you are not going to be responsible for assessing or implementing those alternatives. You can range more widely in your search for alternatives because the reality test is not so strong. It is enough that your alternative 'sounds' feasible. It is enough that the benefits offered by your alternative seem credible. It is, after all, only an exercise in thinking.

PERCEPTION

The above examples refer to alternatives of action, alternative ways of doings things. For many people, alternatives of perception – ways of looking at things – are even more important. From these alternative perceptions come different actions and reactions.

Most businesses look upon recession as a problem. There is a fall in sales and there may be a need to make redundancies. A few businesses, however, see recession as an opportunity in two ways. The first is that it can be an opportunity to invest in research and even production so when the recession passes you will be better placed than your competitors. The second is that weak competitors will be driven out of the market.

Likewise, when a child misbehaves, this is often seen as disobedience, breaking the rules or rebellion. It may also be seen as a sign of an entrepreneurial spirit.

A hobby may be seen as time taken away from more useful studies. A hobby may also be seen as an area for achievement. With a hobby you rate yourself – it is not what the teacher says that matters.

A person seems very jealous of you. Can you see that as flattery?

Immigrants can be seen as a drain on national resources. Immigrants can also be seen as an injection of new energy into a nation.

Perhaps the two most important philosophical statements ever made were made by Henry Ford and Groucho Marx.

When Henry Ford was initiating mass production, he said to his customers: 'You can have any colour you like so long as it is black.' The actual reason for this is that other paints took much longer to dry and so delayed the production process. In real life, what it means is that if what you want is exactly what is available, then you can be very happy.

Groucho Marx famously said: 'I would not want to belong to any club which would accept me as a member.' Presumably he meant that any club which would accept him as a member was not worth joining. In real life, his comment means that if what you want is, by definition, impossible then you are not very likely to be happy.

Every person can place himself or herself along the spectrum between these two remarks. In the end it is a matter of perception.

A different perception is not necessarily a better perception. It may even be worse. But a different perception shows that it is possible to look at something in a different way. It also suggests the possibility that other people have this different perception.

In the UK, going bankrupt is a disaster with a strong social stigma attached to it. In the USA it is viewed as extra, and perhaps necessary, business experience.

When I wrote a book on success and interviewed various people who had been successful in their fields, the attitude taken by some in the UK was that these people might have cheated. In the USA there was admiration of the success and interest in how it had been achieved.

Perceptions vary for any number of reasons: background; culture; values; or personal experience.

Seeking out alternative perceptions is a great deal harder than looking for alternative courses of action. It is very hard to imagine how anyone could look at the situation in a different way from you.

Say, for example, someone suggests painting a red stripe on the car of a person who had committed a traffic offence such as speeding. This would both shame that driver and also warn other drivers to be wary of him or her. At first this seems a good idea. But there could be another perception. Some drives may want to collect as many stripes as possible to show how 'macho' they are. There might even be competition amongst young men to have the most stripes. What is more, people could paint their own red stripes. So committing traffic offences might be seen as 'visible achievement'.

ALTERNATIVE VALUES

It is always very difficult to understand alternative values. How can anyone really hold values which are different from your own? (See also Chapter 12.)

In the West there is a big emphasis on individualism and the ego. You achieve. You fail. You are to be rewarded. You are to be punished. It is the same ego throughout the day. Society is seen as a structure which permits individuals the freedom to achieve their potential and to contribute to society.

In Japan the emphasis is on the group. You fit in. You do not stand out. As in an archway, each stone fulfils its function but does not stick out to disturb the smooth profile of the arch. Achievement means fitting in to the pattern of the group. There is not a single ego throughout the day. During the day a man would be a good 'business man'. During the evening there is a different grouping and he might be a 'social man' having drinks with friends and going to girlie bars. Then he returns home and is a good 'family man'. These are different people linked only by having the same name and the same clothes, etc.

When a Japanese person commits suicide owing to some failure or disgrace it is not a loss of face. It is that that person has fallen out of the group ego and technically no longer exists. Suicide is just tidying up.

The Chinese love gambling. Is this because of their obsession with money? Perhaps not. Chinese 'religion' is quite different from western versions with their gods and saints. In Chinese culture there is an emphasis on fortune, spirits and superstition. When a person is gambling, he or she is really 'in conversation' with the spirits. If that person wins then the spirits are smiling at him or her. When the person loses, the spirits are frowning and you do not want to leave the gambling table on a frown.

In some cultures honour and trust are very important values and come before all others in business. In other cultures pragmatism and 'being smart' seem higher values and 'what you can get away with' is respected.

Some people value privacy. Others prefer publicity and being noticed. Some people like attention. Others shun attention. Some people like peace. Others prefer excitement. Some like stability. Others like change.

GENERATING ALTERNATIVES

Where do alternatives come from?

Let's take a well-known alternative. When you decide to go out to eat in the evening, there are several alternative restaurants that you might choose.

The first step is to bring to mind the known alternatives. If there are none or you have exhausted these, then you need to generate new alternatives. There are some basic approaches to generating fresh alternatives.

The first approach is to find an existing way of doing something and then to identify the concept (see Chapter 9).

Then you ask: What other way might there be of carrying out this concept?

There is a suggestion that prices should be lowered to increase sales. What is the concept here? It could be 'more perceived value'.

How else could this concept be delivered? We could give more volume for the same price. There might be coupons which gave discounts on other goods. There might be free giveaway items with purchased goods. There could be an extra service such as free insurance. There could be a longer guarantee. There could be a 'cash-back' refund.

A Cadillac dealer in California once told me that when the stock market was doing well people were reluctant to buy a Cadillac because they would rather have their funds in the market. So instead of a normal discount I suggested a way of buying the Cadillac *and*, simultaneously, having the funds in the stock market. The purchaser would indicate some shares. The dealer would then note the rise in price of the shares over a year (some determined period). The dealer would then refund to the purchaser the profit that would have been made on those shares. There might be a cut-off limit. In this way the funds were virtually invested in the market – with the advantage that any fall in value of the shares would be ignored.

This method works well for alternatives of action. For alternatives of perception other methods might be needed.

You can seek to see the situation from the point of view of other parties. If gas prices are raised, what might be the

perception of: drivers; bus companies; trucking companies; oil companies; gas stations; out-of-town restaurants;
or the police?

For the idea of arranged marriages what might be the
perception of: less attractive people; people living in isolation; older people; divorced people; or marriage brokers?

Another approach is to take the opposite of the usual
perception. The usual perception might be that harsher
punishments would reduce the rate of crime. Another
perception is that crime might become more violent in
order to eliminate witnesses. Spending longer in prison
might turn a casual offender into a more serious offender.
Courts might be reluctant to secure convictions if the sentence was known to be harsh.

Manners are generally perceived to be a good thing. So
you seek to see in what way manners could be perceived
as being bad. Manners can be learned and need not be
sincere. People can learn manners and then fool other
people. If everyone can act out the manners, how do you
know when someone is a genuinely considerate person?
You may not come to change your view of manners. But
you might realise that manners may hide insincerity.

In order to see alternative values you need to scan
through a whole list of possible values. There are personal
values. For example: importance; being noticed; self-
esteem; prestige; attention; being honoured; being
admired; loyalty. Then there might be material values:
money; prospects of promotion; new contacts; publicity;
or endorsement.

Cultural values are much more difficult if you have no experience of a particular culture and therefore no insight into that culture. You can always ask a direct question: What are the values here? Why is this important to you?

POSSIBLE

The importance of 'possible' has been mentioned in Chapter 2 (see page 22). The progress of science has not come about through certainty but through the use of 'possible' hypotheses. It is said that Chinese science and technology, which was far ahead of the West two thousand years ago, fell behind because of the failure to develop the hypothesis. An hypothesis is not proved until it is proved. Right up to that point it is only 'possible'. But this 'possible' guides our search for new evidence and allows us to design experiments.

> *A detective uses an hypothesis to imagine a possible cause of the crime and then works forward through that hypothesis.*

Alternatives of action and of ideas are about the future. We cannot be certain if a course of action or an idea will work out in practice. Success might be probable or merely possible. But once the idea has been put forward it can be examined and even tried out in a test situation.

Alternatives of explanation and perception, however, are about the present and the past. What caused this? How is this being perceived? Once again proof may not be easy so we have to start off by working with the 'possible', from which we seek to move on to the probable and then the certain.

When possibility becomes too remote it becomes fantasy. This can still have a value, either as a provocation to new thinking or merely to liven up the discussion.

ALTERNATIVES **SUMMARY**

1 Looking for alternatives is a very important activity of a beautiful mind.

2 Without alternatives we have rigidity and complacency.

3 Because we have an adequate way of doing something does not mean that there might not be a much better way. If we try we can find that better way.

4 'Better' may be defined differently according to the values of the situation.

5 There is the willingness to look for alternatives. Then there is the generation of alternatives. Finally there is the assessment of alternatives and a choice.

6 To be chosen a new way of doing something must show clear benefits over the existing way.

7 There can be alternative perceptions or ways of looking at something. These can lead to different judgements or actions.

8 There can be alternative sets of values determined by experience, culture and personality.

9 Alternatives of action can be generated by finding the operating concept and then seeking other ways of carrying out that concept.

10 Alternatives of perception are found by trying out different points of view or by deliberately creating a different perception and seeking to justify it.

11 Alternative values are found by scanning through a range of values – or asking questions.

12 For alternatives, possibility is enough to begin with. We then seek to work forward from the possibility framework to approach certainty.

11 🌴 emotions and **feelings**

Using the coding of the six hats, this is now red hat stuff (see page 93). How do emotions and feelings come into thinking? Is thinking not supposed to be cold and unemotional? What is the connection between emotions and feelings and having a beautiful mind?

If we had no emotions and feelings it would be very difficult to make decisions or choices. Logic, and thinking itself, are only ways of presenting the world so that we can apply our values through our feelings.

Imagine you are in a business meeting and a plan is put forward. One person sees the plan as increasing the profits, increasing his personal prestige and chance for promotion. Another person, who is not interested in promotion, sees the plan as risky, hassle and more work for him. Objectively, the plan is the same for both people but the feelings are different. As a result one person supports the plan enthusiastically, but the other person fights the plan.

Emotions and feelings are the way we apply values to a situation. Our sense of values arouses our feelings, which then become emotions if they are strong enough. (Values themselves are covered in Chapter 12.)

How do emotions and feelings affect thinking?

At the end of a meal you can have a wonderful dessert, which completes the meal. But if you have the sweet dessert at the beginning then your meal may be ruined. It is much the same with emotions and feelings. It all depends where they come in.

SELECTIVE PERCEPTION

A husband suspects that his wife is having an affair. Whenever she is out shopping or with friends he suspects she is meeting her lover. When she returns, his suspicions cause his perception to pick out those things which reinforce his mistrust: Where are the goods she bought if she went shopping?

A wife finds out that her husband is indeed having an affair. She is very upset with him and thinks back over all the details of their married life, picking out minor incidents which 'prove' he never really loved her.

Both examples illustrate 'selection perception'.

A prosecutor in court will select certain pieces of information to suggest a witness is unreliable.

A portrait artist will select and exaggerate those features which seem to show the sitter's personality.

A sociologist will select those aspects of behaviour which support a pre-conceived theory about a particular society.

If you are looking for oranges in a supermarket, your eyes will pick out oranges. If you are looking for breakfast cereal, your eyes will select cereal.

In exactly the same way, our emotions and feelings will 'direct our attention' (see pages 49 and 77) and will pick out what we expect to see. Our perception is rarely objective, it is usually selective.

It is not as if we see everything clearly and then emphasise what our feelings tell us to be important. Our feelings act as a filter so we only see what our feelings let us see. The main danger of strong feelings and emotions, therefore, is that they control our perception. We can no longer see clearly when our perception is controlled in this way.

There is something of a dilemma here. Feelings can control our perception. Yet without feelings we would not be interested in perceiving anything at all.

We do need feelings to direct and broaden our attention. But if the feelings are too strong they restrict and narrow our attention.

Without feelings people would be robots and that would not be much fun. But unrestrained feelings and strong emotions are not much fun either.

Just as a coachman learns how to control a team of six horses so we need to learn how to 'manage' feelings so that we enjoy them and do not get carried away by them. If all the horses bolt, the carriage gets wrecked.

CHOICE

You are offered a choice of holiday. The price is the same in each case. The duration is the same. You can also choose the timing in each case:

a cruise down the Danube on a boat
a stay in the best hotel in Venice
Rio at Carnival time
Bora Bora tropical island near Tahiti
a Caribbean cruise

Which holiday would you choose? There is no skiing holiday or musical festival, which might suit your particular interest. It might be difficult to make a logical choice since the price, duration and timing are the same. In the end you choose the holiday which 'feels' best. This is an emotional choice, and after you have made the choice you may seek to rationalise it. 'That is the holiday I am least likely to have otherwise', for example.

Ultimately all choices and decisions are made on the basis of feelings and emotions. Even when things seem very logical there is still an emotional basis. Suppose you see a garment at one price in one shop and at a lower price in another shop. Surely your choice of the cheaper version is totally logical? Yet there are many underlying feelings:

you do not like to be cheated
you feel it is clever of you to have found a bargain
you look forward to telling your friends about it
you do not like wasting money
you have a sense of achievement

Even when it seems obvious that we should be doing the 'right thing' there are still underlying feelings. There might be the fear of being found out. There might be a sense of guilt. There might even be laziness because doing the wrong thing can be more hassle. We may not want to break a moral principle because this will make decisions more difficult for us in the future.

It is useful to be aware of the emotional basis for decisions and choices. It is extremely difficult to hold back emotions and feelings and only to exercise them at the final point of choice or decision.

ADJECTIVES

Adjectives are usually subjective. Adjectives tell us the subjective feelings of the speaker. When someone uses a lot of adjectives then he or she feels strongly about something. (See also pages 19 and 70.) Unfortunately, subjective adjectives add nothing at all in terms of logic. Objective adjectives do have a place. That 'heavy' case might strain your back, for instance.

On the other hand, 'that marvellous case really suits your style'. All that means is that the speaker thinks that case suits your style. This may be flattering but does not say much about the case itself.

The English language has a number of adjectives to describe people who do things in an unconventional and even innovative way: sly; devious; cunning; crafty; wily. All these have a rather strong negative element. Why is this? Probably because in past times the English class system insisted on things being done in the 'proper' manner. Gentlemen did not try to do things in a faster or 'better' way. An innovative approach was not to be encouraged – you would never know where it might end!

Adjectives tell a lot about people and cultures.

Adjectives are also the simplest and most convenient way to express feelings.

That behaviour is barbaric.
That behaviour is primitive.
That behaviour is so elegant.
That behaviour is so revealing.

Sometimes, by inserting just one adjective at the right point, you can indicate your feeling about the matter. In a discussion on British royalty, for example, someone might insert the adjective 'quaint' at one point. This conveys a lot of feeling. The person is not anti-royalty. The person does not see a real need for royalty. The person sees value in royalty as an amusement. The person thinks of royalty as an interesting relic from the past.

In a discussion on justice let us say that someone inserts the adjective 'slow'. The feeling is that while there may be nothing wrong with the justice delivered, the whole process is cumbersome and inefficient and can drag on for months and years. This slowness is seen as a real negative with no redeeming features. There are times when 'slow' may be used as an objective adjective (the 'slow' train to London) and there are times, as above, when it is used as a subjective adjective to indicate feeling (this is much 'slower' than it really should be).

Someone who is against capital punishment will need to use adjectives in order to show that capital punishment conflicts with his or her values. The adjectives used might be: primitive; cruel; barbaric; or uncivilised. This is because the objection is directly based on a value system. There is little logic except to argue whether or not capital punishment does serve as a deterrent.

FIRST REACTION

When you first hear an idea or a proposition, your first reaction is likely to be based on a feeling or emotion. For example:

I would not be comfortable with that.
I don't like that at all.
That is very unfair.

Those sort of comments are different from:

I don't think that would work in practice.
I do not see the benefit of your idea.
It would be dangerous to do that.

These are also expressions of feeling, but they are intuitive feelings or guesses as to the merit of the idea in terms of whether it would work out or not. You can dislike an idea in itself whether it works or not.

You can also like an idea but have doubts about whether it would work.

Does it make sense to give a first reaction or should you wait silently until you have heard the whole idea and even asked questions to clarify it (see Chapter 7)?

It all depends on the purpose of the discussion and the setting. If it is a serious discussion then it would be better to listen carefully, ask probing questions, consider all the factors and then express an opinion.

In most situations the early expression of feelings adds liveliness to the conversation. There is even a communication advantage. If the person putting forward the idea gets early feedback as to how the idea is being received then he or she can react to this. It may be that the idea is being misunderstood, so there is a need to explain it more carefully. It may be that the listener has too quickly put the idea into a standard 'box' where it does not fit so there is a need to get it out of the 'box'.

Whenever I talk about the need to teach thinking in schools, listeners always assume I am talking about judgement thinking (critical) because that is all they know. So I have to make a strong effort to indicate that I am talking about thinking in the real world – and this is mainly perceptual.

People with expressive faces do not need to say anything in order to indicate a first reaction. The expression on their faces says it all. Salespeople hate having to deal with people with impassive faces which show no feeling at all. How do you know you are getting anywhere? How can you tell which points are hitting home? How can you assess the level of interest? How can you do any of these things without that immediate feedback?

So, on the whole, the early expression of feelings and emotions is not a bad thing.

POSITIONING

In a controversy, where do you want to position yourself? Do you want to be on this side? Or on that side? Or do you want to appear outside the controversy and above it all?

It is a matter of being honest. If your feelings and emotions at the moment place you on one or other side of a controversy, then you need to show where you stand.

Because you have indicated where you stand does not mean that you are going to battle it out with primitive argument. You can still explore both sides of the issue (even using the six hats) in a genuine attempt to understand the other point of view. From this understanding can come the design of a way forward, which reconciles both points of view. Failing that, the points of difference can be clearly laid out.

Indicating where you stand at a given moment does not mean that is where you want to remain. It simply indicates the starting point for the discussion:

'This is where I stand right now. I am willing to help you to convince me to shift.' If both sides could, honestly, think like this, discussions might be much more constructive.

There is a very difficult question that everyone should really ask himself or herself in a discussion or conversation: 'Do I really want to have my mind changed on this matter?' An honest answer is needed.

There is a natural fear that you may have your mind changed by complex 'lawyer type' argument. There is the fear that you may be deceived by false information. These and other fears are natural. At the same time there is a genuine need to be able to listen and to change your mind if necessary.

Some parliaments are constructed so that there are benches on each side of the hall. This means you have to be on the government side or the opposition side. Other parliaments are constructed in a semi-circular or amphitheatre style so there is no definite 'us' and 'them'. It is said that the amphitheatre style encourages small splinter parties and forces government to rely on coalitions, which can be unstable. Whether the physical shape of the hall does make these differences is not important here. What matters is that you do not have to be forced into a position of 'either with us or against us'.

No one can force you into that position. It is your choice. You may agree with an idea up to a point, you may agree with an idea in certain circumstances. You may agree with an idea for a certain section of people. You may agree with an idea with certain modifications (see also page 84).

EMOTIONS AND FEELINGS **SUMMARY**

1   Emotions and feelings are a very important part of thinking.

2   Ultimately, choices and decisions are based on emotions and feelings.

3   Emotions and feelings are our way of linking our values to the situation.

4   Strong emotions or feelings may limit our perception. The resulting 'selective perception' only allows us to see what fits our feelings.

5   Even the most apparently logical of choices may, in the end, depend on feelings. There is a range of subtle feelings involved.

6   Adjectives are usually subjective and tell more about what their user is feeling than about the matter itself. Beware of adjectives used to make a point in place of logic or information.

7   In a very serious discussion you may want to listen first, and ask questions, before showing your feelings.

8   In all other cases there may be a point in expressing your feelings early as this provides useful feedback to the speaker.

9   In a controversy you should show your true position: on one side or the other, or above it all.

10 Your revealed position is where you start from and you may shift from it.

11 You do not have to be for or against an idea. You may like the idea under certain conditions or with certain modifications.

12 You do need to decide whether you are indeed willing to have your mind changed.

12 🌴 values

Which is the more valuable: an ice cream or a tube of vitamin C tablets? One costs rather more than the other. Vitamin C can have a high medical value and ice cream does not. Does this mean the vitamin tablets are more valuable?

Is the question about value being asked about the items themselves, or in certain circumstances?

The vitamin C tablets could be immensely valuable, for example, if someone had vitamin C deficiency and possibly scurvy. (This was a very serious problem for sailors on long expeditions until Captain Cook (among others) took fresh limes on voyages.) Vitamin C could be very valuable if you had a cold, perhaps.

But if you have an adequate diet that includes good supplies of vitamin C then the extra amount has no value at all and is just excreted.

If you really feel like an ice cream then the enjoyment value is high, as opposed to vitamin C, at that particular moment.

If you were short of money, on the other hand, then the money might be better spent on vitamin C. But perhaps you're feeling flush, in which case you could have the ice cream and buy the vitamin C tomorrow, or when you needed it.

CIRCUMSTANCE

Do values depend on circumstance? The answer is both a yes and a no. There are fundamental values which do not change with circumstance. For example, you are not supposed to murder anyone whatever the circumstances. You are not supposed to tell lies under any circumstances (in truth, philosophers have not yet decided this one). You are not supposed to betray your comrades. You are supposed to keep your word of honour. Such fundamental values are religious, social and cultural and should operate in all contexts.

In law, there may be mitigating circumstances which may lessen the sentence. Nevertheless, a crime has been committed. What about killing in self-defence or in war? Is that not killing made legal through circumstance? The argument would be that it is killing but is not 'murder' since you are not doing it for gain and it is sanctioned.

In other cases the values may not change with circumstances but the priority of values changes.

Imagine you are playing cards and you notice that a friend of yours seems to be cheating. What do you do?

There is the *money* value. Because your friend is cheating you may be losing money.

There is the *moral* value. Should you turn a blind eye to cheating just because the person is your friend?

There is the *friendship* value. Should you humiliate your friend and destroy his reputation?

There is another aspect of the friendship value. Should you let your friend develop the habit of cheating until one day he is caught out on a big scale?

Then there is the uncertainty factor. You are not absolutely sure that he is cheating. If he is not and you accuse him, you risk losing his friendship.

In practice you might seek to end the game and then tell him that someone suspects he is cheating. If you do this you seem to be putting a higher priority on your concern for your friend than on the direct moral values involved.

> *You know that your friend's wife is having an affair. Should you tell him? Should you tell her that you know? What are the priority values here? Is it your business?*

Let us say there is a discussion on promotion and you are asked your opinion. You know that your friend needs the promotion very badly. But you also know that the rival candidate, whom you do not like, is more qualified and would be a better choice. What do you do?

There is the value of honesty.

There is the value of helping your friend.

There is the value of being fair to the organisation.

In the above case the values seem to be in conflict in the sense that if you follow one value you do not follow another. If you are honest about the promotion you are not helping your friend.

To take another example, you are buying a house. What are the values involved?

Price and the possibility of getting a mortgage
Do your wife and family like the house?
Is it a long commute to work?
Is the house big enough?
What does the house look like?
Will it impress your friends?
What about shopping?
What about schools in the neighbourhood?
What will the re-sale value be?
Is it a smart neighbourhood?
Are the maintenance costs likely to be high?
How much repair and re-decoration is needed?
Do you like the house aesthetically?
Will you need such a big house when the children
*   are gone?*

Are you likely to find anything more suitable?
Are property prices rising?
Can you wait and look around some more?

This list seems long but most readers of this book could add several more factors. The values might fall into some broad categories: appeal; size; price; convenience; and family. All these values might be changed by particular circumstances.

Shortage of money may mean that price became a priority.

The need for schooling for a young family might be a priority.

The size of the house might become a priority if relatives were in the habit of visiting you.

The wishes of your husband or wife might be a top priority if they differed from yours.

If you are a very competitive person the need to show off might become a top priority.

DIFFERENT PARTIES

In any discussion there are at least three sets of values. There are your values – whether you are fully conscious of them or not. There are the values of the other party (or parties) in the discussion. There are the values of people who are not present but who are being talked about (for example, immigrants, executives, teenagers, feminists, children, old people). This last group may itself need to be broken down into sectors.

Do you know anything about the different values involved, other than your own? You can ask questions and raise possibilities. You can assume major values such as the desire for more money and security. Most discussions proceed along the lines that other people's values are not that different from your own. If we were scrupulous about knowing the values involved we would probably find it very difficult to have any discussion at all!

At one time Catholic Spain had the lowest birthrate in Europe. This was surprising since artificial methods of birth control are not permitted by the Catholic Church. What was happening? It could have been that since the standard of living was rising, couples preferred to have a second income rather than more children. The desire of young women to work may have had a similar effect. Maybe the low birthrate was achieved by abstinence. At some point there were probably clashes of value at a personal, Church and even government level.

PERSONAL VALUES

In addition to the core moral and religious values there is also a range of other values that matter to individuals. Many of these are the 'absence' or opposite of 'negative values' (see page 159):

freedom of action and expression – the absence of tyranny
personal security – the absence of crime, violence and
*   intimidation*
attention and recognition – the absence of being ignored
acceptance in the group – the absence of bullying and being
*   rejected*
dignity – the absence of humiliation
happiness – the absence of suffering
enjoyment and interest – the absence of boredom

Readers will be able to extend this list much further. If you suffer from headaches, then the absence of headaches is a real value. If you never have headaches then that absence is not a value.

In several of the above examples the value could exist directly. For example 'recognition' could be seen as a strong value in itself and not just the absence of being ignored.

ORGANISATION VALUES

Any organisation has values related to both the purpose of the organisation and the running of the organisation.

For a business such values might include: profitability; return to shareholders; competitiveness; cost control; efficiency; customer satisfaction; future prospects.

For a political party the values would include: getting votes; public perception; freedom from scandal; known objectives; charismatic leaders; being distinguished from other parties.

For a family the values might be: sense of family; harmony; helping each other; ability to discuss issues.

QUALITY VALUES

Steel should be strong. Glass should be clear. Restaurant service should be fast and exact. Flights should be punctual. Advertising should attract attention. Vegetables should not be over-cooked.

Quality implies that whatever is being done should be done well in the direction that is intended. Having pink steel may be fun and innovative but it is the function of steel to be strong so quality matters in that direction. Waiters may sing opera in the restaurant and that is fun, but the quality of service is what really matters.

Quality is to do with intention and with expectation. What is intended with a product or service? What is the expectation from a product or service? These two things define what quality should provide.

INNOVATION VALUES

It is difficult to demand innovation. Yet this is what happens with fashion, with gadgets and (to a much lesser extent) with motor cars.

Even when innovation is not demanded or expected, it can be appreciated when it happens.

There is a value in tradition and knowing that you can expect what you have always known. There is also a value in innovation both in terms of improvement and also in terms of excitement.

It is said that the great Napoleon had affairs. In a sermon in Notre Dame, the cardinal preached a sermon on marital fidelity, after which Napoleon invited him to the country for the weekend. For breakfast there was pheasant beautifully cooked. For lunch there was pheasant beautifully cooked. For dinner there was pheasant beautifully cooked. For breakfast next morning there was the pheasant again. The cardinal exclaimed: 'This pheasant is truly a magnificent dish – but always pheasant?'

It is said that Napoleon replied: 'Always Josephine?' (His wife.)

In this particular case other values had priority over novelty, for example, fidelity.

ECOLOGY (IMPACT) VALUES

Few things exist in isolation. Whatever we do usually has an impact on other people and on the environment. In its broadest sense, 'ecology' includes all these impact values.

Does a factory's outflow pollute the river? Does closing down a factory in a small town have a serious impact on that town? Does the emission of greenhouse gases contribute to global warming? Does this dam threaten a rare species of frog?

There are many positive and constructive ecology initiatives, but on the whole the emphasis is on avoiding 'damage' to the environment. It is the consciousness and avoidance of 'negative' impact values that matters most.

PERCEPTUAL VALUES

Perception is real even when it is not reality.

Perception is how you see things, and you feel and react according to what you see – regardless of the underlying reality. (See also page 127.)

Perception matters a great deal to a political party. If something is done which is well meaning and important, it has little value if it is perceived to be done through self-interest. The USA contributes magnificently to world peace, but often this is perceived as being in self-interest. Political 'spin doctors' spend their whole time managing perceptions. How does this look? How will this be seen? How could this be perceived?

It is not enough that justice be done, for instance. Justice must be seen to be done. This traditional view of justice indicates very clearly the immense importance of perception.

So perceptual values are those values which convey what is intended. What is intended may not always be the truth. When something bad happens, there might be an attempt to divert perception to some good aspect of the incident. In such a case 'concern for the truth' or honesty as a value would override expedient perceptual values.

When you dress in an attractive way are you trying to deceive people? Seeking to arrange the best perception is not deceit, although at the extremes it could be so.

NEGATIVE VALUES

This seems a contradiction in terms. And it *is* a contradiction in terms, rather like saying 'good bad things'. Yet there is a practical need for such a phrase. We could just use the word 'harm', but when values are being assessed it would be used to treat values as meaning 'impact'. This impact is always in the positive sense unless specified as 'negative' impact.

There might be a long list of negative values in an ecology impact assessment. In the way a corporation treats its staff there may be a long list of negative values. In family relationships many negative values might be identified.

We would not really want to use the word 'negative success' but there may be a need for a term to indicate that someone has done badly in a spectacular way.

Because 'value' is a term of assessment, it does make sense to use the same word for the negative aspects that are assessed. In your mind you can always equate it with 'negative impact'.

VALUES **SUMMARY**

1   Values determine what we like or do not like, values determine our choices and decisions.

2   Fundamental (core) values are not changed by circumstance.

3   The priority of other values will be determined by circumstance. If you are hungry your values will be different from when you are not hungry.

4   There are times when there will be a conflict between different values and a choice does have to be made.

5   In a discussion, there are your values, the values of others taking part in the discussion and the values of the third parties being talked about.

6   There are personal values, many of which are defined as the absence of negative values.

7   There are organisational values both in terms of purpose and the functioning of the organisation.

8   There are quality values.

9   There are innovation values.

10   There are ecology values, which assess the impact of something on the environment in the wide sense and also the narrow sense.

11   There are perceptual values which relate to how something is perceived. How does it look?

12   The term 'negative value' is used to refer to the 'negative impact' of something.

13 ❀ diversions
and off-course

Off-course vehicles are designed to allow you to drive on rough terrain when you choose to leave the road. What do you do in a conversation when it moves 'off course'?

There is a discussion on the economy of Egypt. Somehow the point is raised as to whether Egyptians today are the same race as the ancient Egyptians who built the pyramids. This leads on to Cleopatra.

There is a story about Mark Antony, who, when he was wooing Cleopatra, used to fish in the Nile before dinner. Cleopatra would pay divers to go down and put fish on Mark Antony's hooks, so that when he returned with all these fish she could congratulate him on his sporting ability.

'They don't make women like that any more,' sighs someone, and the conversation now proceeds on to feminism. That is quite a long way from the Egyptian economy.

How should you deal with diversions? Should you cut them off immediately and say: 'We are discussing the

Egyptian economy today – never mind about Cleopatra.'
Or: 'Let's get back to the subject we are talking about.'

Perhaps you should enjoy the diversion, wherever it may lead. Maybe stories about Cleopatra are more interesting than the economy of Egypt today.

PURPOSE

Much depends on the purpose of the discussion. Is this social cocktail party chat or a serious attempt to explore a problem?

A practical rules is as follows: If the purpose of the discussion is serious, if the diversion is not lengthy, and if there is every intention to return to the main focus, then diversions can be permitted – provided there are not too many of them. It would be dull and boring to clamp down hard on any diversion.

If the purpose of the discussion is amusement and interest, then follow the diversions until you find a point that seems of interest to both parties. Pause and explore that point (see page 49). There is no need to suppose that the starting focus is going to be the most interesting one. If you are driving along a road and are not in a great hurry to get to some destination, why not stop to follow interesting side roads? (See also page 73.)

If, however, you change focus too often and too rapidly, then there is not much chance to develop interest in any area. It is like moving from person to person at a party and never pausing long enough to strike up a conversation.

BORING

There are two reasons a conversation can become boring. The first is that no one has anything to say about the subject. The second reason is that what is said is routine, trite and expected. Both reasons are the direct fault of those involved in the conversation or discussion.

Whatever the subject, it should be possible to find something interesting to say. There could be guesses. There could be speculations. There could be questions. (See also Chapter 4.)

You should be able to have an interesting discussion (even if it is rather short) about the mating habits of the hippopotamus. You do not need to be a biologist to do so. On the way you might, as a diversion, mention that the hippopotamus marks its territory by rotating its short tail very rapidly and emptying its bowels at the same time. The excrement is thus scattered over a wide area (when the shit hits the fan).

Does the male hippopotamus have a harem of ladies, rather like a stag or a walrus? Do a male and female pair off for ever or for the season? Is there a 'dominant male' as with chimpanzees? What is the possible model? In exploring the possible model you can bring in your knowledge of other models in the animal kingdom.

Does the female hippopotamus choose the male on the basis of strength or perhaps beauty (as in the bird world)? Is the female faithful or does she have a number of mates?

It is true that for lack of specific information, such a discussion might range rather widely over general zoological behaviour rather than stick specifically to the hippopotamus species. Such a broadening of the focus is inevitable if not much specific information is available.

If only one party has the information on a subject then it is the role of the other party to open up the discussion by asking questions. These can include provocative questions:

Does the hippopotamus mate on land or in the water (which might seem easier)?

Are there any display signals given out by either gender to indicate a readiness for mating?

Does the hippopotamus come into season at regular intervals or only when aroused by a male?

How often do they mate?

The bases for these questions would be taken from familiarity with some other animal area. Questions are also formed by picking up points in what is being said and seeking elaboration around such points.

Listening to a subject about which you are uninformed is potentially more interesting than just repeating what you already know.

CONVENTIONAL

Protest marches shown on television usually show each party with their traditional slogans confronting each other. Unfortunately, there are a lot of conversations and discussions that use the same format. Each party has its fixed and usually conventional views, and each party confronts the other and seeks to make its views prevail.

In spite of what education may claim, this type of argument or debate is not really very interesting. An exchange of views is interesting – but only if each party is genuinely interested in the views of the other.

> *Why do we have different points of view?*
>
> *What is the essence of the difference between our points of view?*
>
> *Are these different points of view based on different values, different experience or different information?*

The difference is between 'battle' and 'explore'.

The repetition of conventional points of view is boring unless there is an effort to reconcile the points of view and to design a way forward: 'These are the standard points of view. Now, how do we advance forward? Is it a matter of one or other of us being "right" or can we make progress?

I once suggested a sign to go on an executive's desk: 'If you never change your mind, why have one?' If you never changed your mind you could just have a sign saying: 'Same thinking as last month, same ideas too!'

In the same way, repetition of standard positions is not so interesting.

There is a need to suggest new ideas. There is a need to open up areas with more doubt and to explore these. The intention should be that, at the end of the conversation, both parties go away with more than they had at the beginning.

In a discussion on 'globalisation' you might have the opinion that workers in emerging markets are being exploited because the wage they are paid is low compared to the final sale price of the product. That is one position.

The other position is that if workers are paid what is a relatively high wage for their own economy, then this is of great benefit to them. If wages were not lower than in developed countries then the work would not have come there in the first place. Would it be better to have high wages but no work?

Both points of view can be argued strongly. An attempt could be made to design ways forward. Either party could suggest such ways forward. The final price of the product could be lowered to reflect the lower wage component, for instance. This would benefit consumers but would put other manufacturers out of business and eventually other workers too. Another idea would be to take some of the profits due to the low wages and to put these into a special 'aid fund' for help in education or health in the district where the work was done.

A new idea may not be acceptable and may not even be feasible. What matters is that the idea is an attempt to go beyond mere repetition of conventional positions.

Does this mean that winning arguments is not important? Exploring the subject honestly and thoroughly and coming to a conclusion is probably more important than just proving your point. If it is important to win the argument, then try to introduce some new considerations. Just repeating the old stuff is indeed boring.

HUMOUR

Humour is a very important part of having a beautiful mind. Humour has several functions:

Humour lightens things up and adds some fun.

Humour is half serious and allows things to be said which might or might not be taken seriously. The listener can choose whether or not to take the suggestion seriously. In this respect humour has the same value as a provocation in lateral (creative) thinking (see page 48).

Humour also allows speculation. Something may not be very likely – but it is just possible. For example: 'Maybe we should have beauty police?'

There is a seaside town in Italy that has beauty police. If you do not look good in a bikini you are not allowed to wear one!

When specific jokes are introduced they should be relevant and make a point. A joke that is just dragged in with no relevance is an irritating intrusion.

Fantasy is a form of humour. Through rather absurd exaggeration a point can be made. If an executive is in the habit of micro-managing everything, you could say he or she wants to know every time someone puts fuel into his or her car. No one would believe that to be true but it does make the point, as does: 'Old Joe would not recognise a new idea even if it wore a bright pink tutu and did handstands in front of him.'

There is the mistaken belief that everything in a serious conversation should be deadly serious. This is not so at all. A totally serious conversation may be so boring that no one remembers what was said. A change of pace and tone make for better understanding and better retention.

ENJOYMENT

You should enjoy the use of your mind and other people's use of their minds. Being right is not the only form of enjoyment. Putting forward new ideas and new insights is enjoyable. So is listening to new ideas and new insights. Finding new ways of looking at something is enjoyable. So is new information.

Conversation is like a dance. It is more fun dancing with someone else: a dance of the mind. If your dancing partner knows the steps it is even more enjoyable. In the same way, if other people know the 'rules' of conversation the process is more enjoyable. If they do not know the rules they may spend the time trying hard to convince you that they are 'right'.

Many people enjoy sport. They enjoy the use of the body for some trivial purpose (like getting a ball into a net). It is the activity that matters – not the purpose. Why should not people enjoy the use of their minds in this 'sporty' way? Why not enjoy the sheer pleasure of thinking? Rodin, in his famous statue 'The Thinker', did thinking a great disservice by showing thinking as heavy and solemn. It can also be light and fun!

DIVERSIONS AND OFF-COURSE **SUMMARY**

1 The main purpose of the discussion will determine whether diversions are acceptable or not. When the purpose is very serious then diversions may be less acceptable.

2 Provided diversions are not too long and that there is a return to the main focus, diversions add enjoyment to any discussion and should be welcomed.

3 A discussion will always be boring if no one has anything to say about the subject. It is important to develop the habit of 'interest', which allows you to find any subject interesting.

4 Where there is not much information, interest can be created by questions and by speculation. There can also be references to known subject areas.

5 Just repeating conventional ideas can also be boring. Doing battle with one set of ideas against another is boring.

6 Where there are strong differences of opinion it becomes interesting to explore the basis for that difference.

7 It may be possible to reconcile opposing views or at least to make clear the actual difference.

8 New ideas are also welcome in any conversation because they are new and provide an escape from the usual thinking. An idea can provide a provocation even if the idea is not feasible.

9 Humour is a very important ingredient and a key feature of the beautiful mind.

10 Humour allows speculation and enables things to be put forward as half serious and half humorous.

11 Humour permits exaggeration and absurdity to make a serious point.

12 Conversation and discussion should be as enjoyable for the mind as sport is for the body.

14 🌴 information
and knowledge

It is impossible to have complete information about everything.

How much information do you need to take part in a conversation? What sort of information should you seek in general in order to equip your mind for a discussion?

These are open-ended questions for which there is no definite answer. When you go away on holiday, how much information do you collect in order to make your choice of destination? Some people might seek to collect detailed information. Others are content with general information about price, weather and entertainment.

HOW MUCH?

How much do you need to know about cloning to be able to have a conversation on cloning?

You may know that a sheep called Dolly was cloned in the UK. You may know that a cat called CC was cloned in the USA. You have a hazy view of what cloning is about. If you are talking to an expert on cloning, therefore, your side of the conversation is intelligent listening, questions and learning:

In what way would the cloned person be identical to the cell donor?
Would the personalities be the same?
Could the cloned person have children?
If the donor cell came from an older person, would all that person's cells be old?
How many people could be cloned from one cell?
What would be the legal position in terms of inheritance?

It is not difficult to generate questions if you want to learn about a fascinating subject. At the same time you want to generate some to-and-fro discussion in order to make it more interesting for the other party. So you might focus on one point that emerges and try to build this up into a two-sided discussion: 'How far would the personality of the cloned person be similar to that of the donor?'

This would open up the whole question about personality depending on genes, upbringing and circumstance.

If you were having the conversation with someone whose ignorance on cloning matched your own, however, you would need to talk in generalities based on the lay view of the process:

Why would you want to be cloned?

Who would want to be cloned?

If the process became available and cheap, what effect would this have on families and on society?

What are the advantages, if any, of human cloning?

If you were to clone a winning race horse would the resulting race horse also be a winner?

If Einstein had been cloned what might the resulting person have been like?

How much you need to know depends on the subject matter. The subject of cloning is so exotic and so fascinating that almost anyone can have a speculative conversation on that subject. But if the subject had been 'orchids' it would be difficult to have a conversation unless at least one person knew quite a lot about orchids.

In any case, you are never really compelled to have a conversation about a subject where your knowledge is very low or even non-existent. If others are holding the conversation, you can take part by listening and asking the occasional question.

A bad strategy is to pretend you know something about the subject when you actually know very little. You would get found out sooner or later. Such a strategy also prevents you from asking questions which might seem stupid if coming from someone with some knowledge of the subject but acceptable from a person with no such knowledge.

There is no harm in saying: 'I know nothing about that subject, but I am willing to listen and to learn.'

Often people who know a lot about a subject enjoy explaining the subject to an attentive listener. As you, the expert, explain your subject you can receive fresh insights and also find more powerful ways of explaining things.

From time to time the listener should sum up what has been heard. This serves to reassure the speaker that he or she has been understood. It also serves to clarify matters for the listener. (See also page 54.)

THE ZULU PRINCIPLE

You choose a special subject that most people are not likely to know much about. For example, you might choose the Zulus. You now become an expert in that field. You can hold forth on that subject.

You can explain how the Zulu language does not have a word for no. You simply use the word for yes and draw out the syllable to indicate the degree of uncertainty. This is similar to saying: 'Ye-e-e-s' in English to indicate considerable doubt.

You can explain how the Zulu men are very warlike and prance around in leopard skins, but that actually it is a matriarchy and the women control most things. You could then compare this with other cultures such as Japan.

In other conversations that have nothing to do with Zulus you can seek to bring in your specialised knowledge.

There may be two or three areas in which you set out to acquire specialised knowledge. It could be the breeding of Dalmatians or the financial scandals of Tulipmania in the UK. In time you will become very skilled in applying lessons or principles from these exotic areas to almost any conversation.

THE MIRROR STRATEGY

A very well-known management consulting firm is said to use the 'mirror strategy'. The consultants are called in by senior management of a business because of some problem or need to reorganise. The consultants come in and move around the organisation, listening very carefully to what is being said. From what they have heard they put together a report which is then presented to senior management.

Because the consultants are charging a high fee, senior managers now read the report and listen to what is being said. In the past they may not have listened to what people in their own organisation were saying.

This type of consultancy serves a very useful role by reflecting back, as a mirror, what is really already present. It also has to be said that because the ideas pass through the consultants they are in a sense 'validated' by the experienced judgement of the consultants.

In the same way it is possible to listen to what a lot of different people say on a subject and then to put this together to form your own knowledge base, which you are then free to use.

Repeating to one person what you have recently heard from another is perfectly valid. The danger is that if the first person has got it wrong, so too will you.

You may, of course, add your own interpretation or slant to knowledge you have picked up from others. This is exactly what the consultants were paid for doing.

If you have heard people discussing a particular movie, you can repeat the comments even if you have never seen the movie. You might choose to indicate that these were, indeed, remarks you had heard.

KNOWLEDGE INPUT

Where do you get your knowledge input? What do you feed into your mind?

There are the usual information sources: newspapers, books, lectures, other people, the Internet, magazines, or courses. But there needs to be a dual approach. On the one hand there is a general awareness of what is happening in the world. This would usually be obtained through newspapers, news bulletins and the conversation of other people. On the other hand, there are the specialised interest areas (even if not the Zulu principle itself) which you explore in much greater depth – sometimes using the Internet for very specialised information.

When Japanese tourists were asked why they went to Queensland, Australia, 39 per cent said they went 'to cuddle a koala'. Now Queensland has magnificent rainforests and beaches. But if you go back to Japan and say that the landscape was magnificent, that does not mean much at all. However, if you show a photograph or a video clip of yourself cuddling a koala, that means far more. There is an important point arising from this story.

General broad information about a subject may not be as interesting as the tiny quirky items you might have read. Such items are often no more than a small paragraph somewhere in the newspaper. The item might be about two thousand people kissing simultaneously on a bridge in Moscow in order to get into the Guinness Book of Records.

It would be difficult to build a conversation entirely around these 'high interest' items. The items, however, can be door-openers to other discussions. From the Moscow item you can move on to the need to be famous (even for fifteen minutes, as Andy Warhol advised) and what people will do to be mentioned somewhere. You could also explore the strange habit of 'kissing' itself. Is it a way of transferring pheromones?

In any case, such items act like currants in a cake to provide instances of interest in what otherwise might be quite stodgy. So it is always worth building up a repertoire of such items and having them ready for any occasion.

MAKING DO

A good cook can make do with any ingredients. It is not difficult to put together a good meal from unlimited ingredients. It is not difficult to have a great conversation if both parties are fully informed on the subject. But just as a good cook can prepare a meal from any ingredients so a beautiful mind can fashion a discussion from any information base.

You prod and you probe to see where possible areas of interest lie and then you follow through and open up those areas. Some people are boring if left to themselves but in the hands of a skilled conversationalist these people become more interesting than they had ever imagined possible.

There is a need to be pro-active rather than passively reactive. It is not a matter of sitting back and saying, 'Amuse me.' It is more a matter of working jointly to see what can be made of a limited knowledge base.

Feelings, values and speculation are never limited by a poor knowledge base. Imagination is unlimited. Whether the ideas that emerge are realistic is another matter, but the discussion can be great fun.

Imagine a conversation about heaven. No one has any specialised information. Everyone has some vague ideas about angels and music. So, like Dante, you are free to exercise your imagination and to discuss what you create.

INFORMATION AND KNOWLEDGE **SUMMARY**

1 You do not need full and complete information about a subject in order to discuss that subject.
2 If the other person has more information than you do, listen intelligently and ask questions.
3 You can also pick out some point of interest and have a two-way conversation around that particular point.
4 There is no point in pretending to know more about a subject than you really do. Ignorance is actually a stronger position.
5 With the Zulu principle you become an expert in some exotic subject area and talk about this whenever you can.
6 Even when you are not directly talking about Zulus you can bring in points and lessons from that area.
7 With the 'mirror strategy' you do a lot of listening and then feed back what you have heard. You can repeat as your own knowledge collected from many different sources.
8 In organising your information input there is a need for a dual strategy. There needs to be a general awareness of what is going on in the world. There also need to be certain areas of deeper interest, which you explore more thoroughly.
9 There may need to be a conscious effort at information collecting. What comes along by chance may not be sufficient.

10 It is useful to build up a small repertoire of 'high interest' items that may be quirky. These serve to spice up a dull conversation. They can also act as starting points for many different conversations.

11 A good conversationalist creates an interesting discussion out of whatever information is available.

12 Even when there is very little information, imagination and speculation can provide the basis for discussion.

15 🌴 opinion

Do you have the right to have an opinion?

When do you have the right to have an opinion?

Who has the right to have an opinion?

At one extreme we can have a person who knows very little about a subject and yet comes out with a strong opinion on that subject.

At the other extreme is someone who is well informed and has thought a lot about the subject, but is unable to express an opinion.

An opinion is a sort of stew of information, perceptions, feelings and values, cooked together within a particular culture.

WHY HAVE OPINIONS?

You might as well ask, 'Why have people?'

It is possible to imagine a discussion in which no one has an opinion. There is a mutual exploration of the subject. At some point, however, values need to get attached and that attachment results in an opinion.

There may be opinions which are very strongly held. There may be tentative opinions which are a sort of 'holding position' until a better opinion forms. There may be opinions which are held quite firmly but are still open to change.

You can contemplate an extensive menu in a restaurant but at some stage you have to order a particular dish – even if you are torn between two.

A beautiful mind is capable of forming opinions and is not afraid to do so. At the same time, the beautiful mind is always conscious of the basis for that opinion. Furthermore, any opinion held is open to change. This is not unlike a scientific hypothesis. The hypothesis is definite and usable – otherwise no experiments could ever be designed. Yet the hypothesis is only 'provisional' and the scientist is always seeking to form a better one (see also pages 46 and 134).

If you are more fully informed on a subject than someone else, is your opinion more valid? Not necessarily. Perception and values are also important. There may indeed be a definite piece of information that shows another opinion is more valid than yours.

For example, if you believed that in an arranged marriage the partners were 'forced' to go through with the marriage, you might have an opinion that was strongly against this custom. If, however, you were told that either partner could simply turn down the offer, then your opinion might change.

PROVOKING OPINIONS

There are some people whose style it is to put forward as a strong opinion an opinion they do not really hold that strongly. The purpose of this is to provoke other people into argument and discussion. There is merit in this strategy, but it is also risky. You can easily get the reputation of being full of strong opinions based on nothing very much. You might wish to be treated as a sort of 'jester' but might end up being seen as a light-weight or air-head.

In order to get a discussion going you might want to offer a provocative opinion. There is no reason, however, why you should not signal it as such: 'Suppose I put forward this provocative opinion . . .' Or: 'This is not what I really feel, but suppose someone offered this opinion . . .' Or: 'Here is an opinion to get the discussion going . . .' (See also page 48.)

EXERCISE

Here is an exercise in instant opinions. For each of the following subject areas see what instant opinion you might offer. Then, for each of the subject areas, put forward a deliberately provocative opinion, which might be very far from your real opinion:

the fight against terrorism
school vouchers

the homeless
large shopping malls
universities
living together before marriage
unlimited immigration
owners' responsibility for dog violence
sports idols
feminism
aid to poor countries
cosmetic surgery
legalisation of prostitution
living in the country

POINT OF VIEW

If you are standing on the top of a mountain, you have one point of view. If you are standing in the valley below you have another. If you are standing in the middle of a vast plain (perhaps Manitoba) you would again have a different point of view.

If you are a white middle-class woman, aged forty, living in an affluent suburb, you have one point of view. If you are a teenage girl living in a rough neighbourhood you would have another point of view.

The difficult question is this: How personal should your opinion be?

It is difficult because the best opinion would be based on your experience, values, culture and point of view. At the same time, this would be a rather limited point of view.

If people only based their opinions on their own point of view, democratic politics could never work. On the whole, the people in power are rather more affluent and comfortable than many of the people for whom they are making decisions.

So it would seem necessary to consider other possible points of view. This is easier to say than to do. How easy would it be to consider the point of view of a homeless drug addict? It would be easy enough to suppose that such a person would need: shelter; support; medication; and rehabilitation. Although that sounds reasonable it may actually be far from the point of view of that person, who may just want easier access to drugs at a lower price.

At this point we get into the rather tricky area of deciding what is best for other people, even if this is not what they themselves want. It may need to be done.

When you vote in an election you vote for 'your opinion'. You do not vote on behalf of the majority of people who might have a point of view different from your own. If each of those people also votes for his or her opinion then democracy will take that opinion into account.

Is an ordinary discussion more like an election, or more like being in government? If the former, then you are fully justified in speaking directly from your point of view. Perhaps you would prefer not to pay more taxes even if the money was going to welfare, for example. If a discussion is more like government, then you might, on the other hand, want to consider what is best 'for most people' or 'for the nation as a whole'.

The question is not an easy one because you might offer a much better opinion from your point of view rather than taking everyone else into account.

There was a time when the USA appeared to be isolationist and not too bothered about the rest of the world. That seems to have changed dramatically.

The first US international policing operation might have been when the US sent a naval squadron into the Mediterranean to attack the Barbary corsairs (pirates) in the Tripolitan wars (1801 to 1805). That is how the mention of Tripoli gets into the battle song of the marines!

Are you a citizen of the world, of your country, or of your town or suburb? You may want to offer different opinions according to your stated point of view:

This is my personal opinion . . .
Looking at this from a national point of view, this is my
    opinion . . .
From the point of view of humanity and human values, this
    would be my opinion . . .

It might be rather cumbersome if everyone offered multiple opinions. So you would try to merge the opinions into one personal opinion. If not, then you should signal the point of view.

CHANGING OPINIONS

This is another key aspect of the beautiful mind. To refuse to change an opinion is an indication of a rigidity which is far from beautiful.

How long should you hold on to an opinion? What would get you to change your opinion?

There are two basic types of change. The easiest is where you modify the opinion you hold – you might tone it down. The more difficult change is where you reverse your opinion or accept someone else's opinion.

Changing an opinion is never a sign of weakness. On the contrary, it is one of the few ways of demonstrating the open thinking that is essential in a beautiful mind. What better demonstration of open objective thinking than to change your opinion. It is natural to defend your opinion. To change your opinion goes much further.

If everyone were ready to change opinions, then discussions would be much more constructive and much less like ego battles.

NEW INFORMATION

New information is possibly the most powerful cause for a change of opinion. It is also the most acceptable.

If you hold the opinion that in criminal cases the defendant is poorly represented, and then you learn that 95 per cent of criminal cases are settled by plea bargaining, your point is much weakened. You might, of course, argue that the accused chooses plea bargaining because he or she knows that the representation in court is likely to be poor.

In Sweden 50 per cent of babies are born to unwed mothers. Your opinion might be that this represents a break-down of families, and poor moral standards. If you were now informed that many of the mothers did subsequently marry the father of their child, your opinion might change.

If you held the opinion that crime in New York was increasing and then someone told you that the statistics showed that it was actually decreasing, you might change your opinion.

LESS COMPLETE

There is always a huge temptation to make sweeping generalisations. (See also pages 9, 21, 57 and 62.)

'All politicians are corrupt. All of them have their price' sounds much more important than: 'I suspect there might be some corrupt politicians.'

In the course of a discussion your generalisation might gradually diminish along the following lines:

all politicians are corrupt
most politicians are corrupt
the majority of politicians are corrupt
many politicians are corrupt

some politicians are corrupt
a few politicians are corrupt
there are corrupt politicians

Where you finally stop along that spectrum depends on the evidence, and opinions, put before you – and your willingness to listen.

The change from 'all' to 'most' and even to 'many' is not so difficult. Moving beyond that is difficult because it destroys the whole opinion.

VALUE CHANGE

Opinions can be changed if you realise – or if it is suggested to you – that the values you are using may not be universal.

It may be that other cultures put a higher value on compatibility than on romantic love. So your opinion on arranged marriages is purely personal.

You can insist that other people should have the same values as you have, and yet come to realise that they do not.

Then there are people who hold certain values in the abstract: in general or for other people. But when it becomes local or personal, the values change.

Take a country which is seen as a role model in liberal thinking and caring. But when Somali refugees were placed in that country they were not welcomed. The expression NIMBY expresses this. You may be much in favour of a new garbage dump or wind farm, but you are not in favour if it is to be in your back yard.

In politics the expression is NIME. This means that a politician is all in favour of certain changes but not at election time: Not In My Election.

COMPARISON AND DIFFERENCE

As mentioned at so many other points in this book, there is much merit in laying opinions down alongside each other. Both opinions are expressed honestly and clearly.

You can then see the points of overlap and agreement.

You can then see the points of difference. Sometimes the difference may be major and at other times the difference may be slight.

You can then seek out the source or origin of the difference (different information, different experience, different perception, different values).

You can seek to reconcile the differences by modifications to both opinions or by exchanging further information.

If you cannot achieve a 'joint opinion' you can still agree on the points of difference. Usually the difference is due to a different guess as to what might happen if some change or intervention is put in place.

For example: 'I believe that language is inadequate to convey complex situations and that if we had a universal "situation code" we could immediately communicate the situation. You believe that language is perfectly capable of doing this if used properly. I may agree with you there but then I feel that only a few people would use language so "properly" and therefore the codes would make life easier for most people.'

OPINION **SUMMARY**

1 To have a strong opinion that is based on very little is one extreme. To refuse to have an opinion when you are well informed is the other extreme. It is best to be somewhere in between.

2 An opinion arises from information, values, feelings and experience put together in a local culture.

3 It can be useful to put forward a strong opinion as a provocation but it is best to signal what you are doing.

4 Opinions are based on a point of view which is the set of circumstances in which you are placed.

5 You may choose to put forward an opinion based on your very personal point of view and leave it to others to do likewise.

6 You might want to put forward an opinion on what might be best 'in general' or for everyone.

7 You should signal the nature of the opinion: personal or more general.

8 A beautiful mind is always ready to change opinions. This is a characteristic of a beautiful mind.

9 An opinion may be changed by new information.

10 An opinion may be reduced from a broad generalisation to a less complete form.

11 An opinion may be changed through acceptance of other values.

12 Different opinions should be laid alongside each other. There is then an attempt to explore the basis of the difference and effect a reconciliation. If not, there can be agreement as to the points of difference.

16 🌴 interruption

When is it your turn to speak?

Can you wait until it is your turn to speak?

Is interruption necessary, or just bad manners?

If someone is continually interrupting you, this breaks the thread of what you are trying to say. Instead of there being a smooth logical progression there are now separated islands of comment. It may become difficult to link them into a coherent whole.

Imagine an artist painting a picture. Standing nearby is someone who is continually interrupting the artist's work. The interrupter may make suggestions as to how something should be painted. The interrupter may criticise what is being done. The interrupter may even seize the paint brush and insert his or her own version. The artist is not likely to be pleased. The painting may suffer from these interruptions. Interrupting a conversation is rarely as serious as that but interruption is still an interruption.

In general, interruption is not something to be encouraged. There may, however, be occasions where interruption is useful and even necessary.

MY TURN

A conversation is not a lecture or a monologue. It is supposed to be a dialogue and an interaction. If one person goes on and on, this gives little opportunity for other people to express their views and opinions.

When you are a guest on a television show, the presenter indicates by his or her facial expression that it is time you shut up. If the guest goes on and on, that could be boring for the audience and the presenter does not get enough 'air time'.

In a normal conversation it is rather more difficult to express impatience facially without seeming to be very rude.

You can try to make tentative interruptions, which are designed just to indicate that you want a chance to speak: 'Yes . . .' 'But . . .' 'I think . . .'

Such interjections rarely work, however. Someone who is used to going on and on is also used to ignoring attempts to cut him or her short.

I once organised a meeting at UNESCO in Paris. There were several very eminent speakers who had important things to say. Each had been allotted fifteen minutes – which may not have been long enough. The first speaker went on for forty-five minutes. Everyone was getting very impatient. So I organised a signalling system for subsequent speakers.

I placed three Coca-Cola bottles on a table visible to everyone sitting around. When a speaker had five minutes left, I would get up and remove one of the bottles. When the speaker's time was up I would remove the second bottle. When the speaker had over-run by five minutes and really needed to shut up, I removed the last bottle. The system worked well for the remainder of the meeting.

There is a story of an English squire who tired of the long sermons of the vicar in the village church. The squire was seated in a pew just in front of the pulpit. When the sermon started the squire put three five-pounds notes (a large sum of money in those days) on the bench in front of him. This money was going to be given to the vicar at the end of the service. Every ten minutes the squire would remove one of the notes and put it back in his pocket. If the sermon lasted longer than thirty minutes the donation was all gone.

In the Conversation Club mentioned at the end of this book (see page 226) there is a formal mechanism for indicating that it is time to shut up and give someone else a chance to talk.

As you impatiently await your turn to contribute, you come to realise how annoying it is when someone goes on and on. So when it is your turn to speak, you should now be conscious of that and restrain yourself from doing the same.

Instead of making a speech (Fidel Castro goes on for four hours), confine yourself to making one point at a time. If you want to mention several points, do so as headings and then come back to them later.

Some people signal that they want to make four points and use this to prevent anyone interrupting until they have completed, in detail, all four. It is enough to mention the points and then come back to them later.

EGO INTERRUPTIONS

Most interruptions are ego-driven. You want to be noticed. You want to get attention. You want to be important. You want to show you are smarter than the speaker.

There are some people who interrupt the whole time on this basis. They are worse than irritating – they are infuriating. Everyone around gets very fed up with that person. It is only fair to let the speaker develop the point he or she is trying to make.

As a speaker, or even as an onlooker, you can be abrupt in cutting off such interruptions: 'I am going to finish what I am saying.' Or: 'Let her finish what she is saying.'

AMPLIFYING INTERRUPTIONS

Such interruptions are meant well. They are intended to enlarge and amplify the point being made: 'And what is more . . .'

The interruption may offer examples from personal experience. The interruption may offer statistics. The interruption may offer new perceptions. The interruption may seek to apply values.

Amplifying interruptions are usually (but not necessarily)

'supporting' in nature. You agree with the point being made and you want to amplify the point by adding material and comment which support the point. (See also page 55.)

If someone is talking about the matriarchal system in Zulu culture, you may add that this is also the case in other African tribes. These are parallel comments, which neither support nor challenge what is being said.

If the speaker offers an example of the difficulty of judging certain events at the Olympic Games, you may interrupt to give further examples.

If amplifying interruptions are too lengthy, however, they may still destroy the thread of what is being said. There may need to be some self-restraint in not saying everything that could be said at any point.

CHALLENGE INTERRUPTIONS

Challenge interruptions are justified and important, but difficult to deal with.

There are times when someone says something which is plainly wrong. A quote may be attributed to the wrong person. The person may be right but the quote itself may be wrong. If someone said that the town of Nice was in Italy that would be wrong (although it was Italian at one time). If someone said that Muslims were encouraged to have more than one wife, that would be wrong (permitted is not the same as encouraged). If someone said that Bill

Clinton was the thirty-ninth president of the USA that would be wrong.

If the error is small and unimportant you might want to let it pass rather than interrupt with a correction. But if the error was central to the argument you would not want to let it pass. So you interrupt – as politely as possible:

'Are you sure? I thought Nice was in France.'

'I understand that Muslims are permitted, under certain conditions, to have more than one wife. That is not the same as encouraged to do so.'

'I may well be wrong but wasn't Bill Clinton the forty-second president?'

There is another type of challenge where there is no obvious error of fact but there may be an error of logic. Something may not necessarily follow from something else – as claimed. There could be a sweeping generalisation that needs to be challenged, for example (see Chapter 2). The disagreement may be expressed as an interruption or you may wait for an opportunity to voice your disagreement.

Quite often you will want to challenge figures and statistics. This does not mean that you know them to be incorrect. You want to know the source of the statistics. You want to know how recent they are. You may want to know the sample size. You may want to know to which population they apply, for instance.

Challenge always implies: I am not going to let you get away with that.

This is not necessarily an argumentative or 'attacking' challenge. You may genuinely want to be sure of something and ask: 'That is a very important point. Those statistics are very significant. Could I ask where they come from and how recent they are?'

'That is a most interesting point. Whose figures are those?'

IMMEDIATE OR LATER

Sometimes you may feel that it is very important to interrupt at precisely the point where the interruption is needed. You may feel that it is not enough to wait your turn and then make your point in retrospect. In practice you have three choices:

1   *Wait until you get to speak and then make the challenge, correction or amplification. This is easier to do in two-person conversations because your turn will come soon. In multi-party conversations it may be so long before you get to talk that the point will seem irrelevant.*

2   *Interrupt and say all you have to say. The danger here is that if you have a lot to say, your interruption may completely destroy the coherence of the line of thinking that is being put forward. It is unrealistic to expect people to remember exactly what was said before the interruption and to carry on from that.*

3   *Make your interruption at the relevant point but do not*

make your full speech. You simply 'signal' the point you will be making later. For example:

I don't agree with you at this point. I shall come back to that later.
I don't think those figures on divorce are correct. I shall tell you why I want to challenge them later.
You could look at it that way. But you could also look at it this way . . .
That is not the only possible explanation. There is another explanation which may be even more likely. I shall come to that later.

The speaker may pause at a point of his or her own choosing to allow you to make your point. Otherwise you will have to wait until you speak again to follow up on what you have promised.

DOUBTS

We have seen that you may interrupt to claim that something is wrong. You may challenge something. You may seek to amplify or support a point.

You can also interrupt to express doubts:

I am never too happy with that argument.
That is the usual explanation given but I sometimes wonder if it is the right one.

We have always believed that it must be so, only because we have not been able to think of another possibility.

> **Proof is sometimes no more than a lack of imagination in thinking of an alternative.**

In the island of Malta there is a huge number of pre-historic Stone Age remains. Indeed, the oldest free-standing man-made structure in the world is in the island of Malta. Among the oldest remains are apparent 'cart tracks' consisting of parallel grooves cut in the rock and extending for some distance.

Because these tracks are reminiscent of a railway line it has always been assumed that they were used for transport of some sort. I doubt that. Before the invention of the wheel there had to be 'linear factories'. This means that you dragged something along a groove to grind it (whether an axe or even corn). So what about the second parallel track? That was for stability – a sort of outrigger. Of course, both tracks could then be functional and both could be used for grinding. This is a serious possibility.

Sometimes it may seem that if you keep silent you are agreeing with the speaker. When this is not so it should not be perceived as such. When everyone is nodding in apparent agreement you may need to interrupt to indicate you feel otherwise: 'I have some doubts about that. I shall explain them later.'

There is agreement, disagreement, difference, doubt and 'unconvinced'. Unconvinced means an open mind which has not yet formed an opinion or judgement.

INTERRUPTION **SUMMARY**

1 Interruptions are generally rude and break the flow of what is being said. So there needs to be a very good reason for the interruption.

2 If someone is simply going on and on, there may be a need to indicate that a conversation is a two-way affair. For the same reason, do not be the person who is going on and on.

3 Interruptions are often 'ego-driven'. Someone wants to be noticed or feel important. Someone wants to show he or she is smarter than the speaker.

4 Amplifying interruptions seek to elaborate around a point by offering further information or examples.

5 Amplifying interruptions can offer 'support' for the point being made or simply offer parallel information.

6 Challenge interruptions are important and often justified.

7 You can point out that something is factually wrong.

8 You can point out errors in logic. You can point out that something does not necessarily follow.

9 You can challenge sweeping generalisations.

10 You can interrupt and seek to make your full point or you can signal that you will make the full point later.

11 You can interrupt to express doubt.

12 When circumstances suggest that silence may be interpreted as agreement with what is being said, you may need to interrupt to indicate otherwise.

17 🌴 attitude

Self-image and attitude usually go together.

If you are the 'clever person' who always has to be right, then you are going to be argumentative and intent on showing others how smart you are. You will choose to attack the tiniest points with which you disagree rather than focus on the main points with which you might agree. You will always challenge the information offered by other people and then seek to top it with information of your own. You will rarely offer new ideas because a new idea is a risk and can be attacked. You would prefer to confine yourself to criticism because this makes you sound superior and does not leave you yourself open to criticism. If an idea is put forward, you will be ready with a 'Yes, but . . .' to show that the idea is not so great after all. You will be reluctant to agree with anyone because agreeing also diminishes your chance of being superior. You may even utter quite ordinary statements as if they were profound philosophic insights. In short, you will enjoy being clever and seeking to impress others with how clever you are.

There is nothing very beautiful about the mind that always has to be right and put other people down. The attitude is win, win and win.

Then there is the attitude of a person who implies that he or she alone is the custodian of 'true human values': 'Never mind the argument. Never mind the information. In the end the true human values must decide the issue.'

If you are such a person, you seize on any opportunity to show that the values you hold are really the deciding issue. Everything else is messing around. There is an arrogance of values here just as there is an arrogance of logic in the first type. There is a suggestion that everything should be decided by feelings and values and intuition. If your heart is in the right place and if you mean well then your judgements and decisions are bound to be right. You alone can see to the heart of the issue. You see arguments only as a way of rationalising wrong positions and seeking to persuade other people of the validity of those positions. There can be no argument with values since you hold the right values. There is not even much need to listen to other people.

The attitude is one of righteousness. You do not have to defend your position because you are right. You are right because you have the right values.

Then there is the person who plays dumb. If you play dumb you can get away with a lot. You do not have to have a position and no one is going to attack your ideas. You can ask the most outlandish questions and get away with it. You are anxious to accept what other people say and eager to agree with them. You are the perfect listener but may not have much to contribute. You may even find people who feel sorry for you. Such people would take your side and build up your point of view or even provide you with an opinion. You will not need to do all your own thinking.

That attitude is one of eager helplessness and it can be both attractive and effective.

Then there are people who are very, very reasonable. In fact, they are so reasonable they can never commit to a position because they always see the other position so clearly. They accept all points that are offered without argument. Everything is possible. Nothing is certain. Very little is even probable. There do not seem to be any values or feelings and if they are present they are so balanced they cannot form the basis for any choice or decision. The overall effect is that of a map which shows many routes but never shows one particular route.

The attitude is that of the triumph of reason over emotion.

Then there is the bully. For this person, conversation is only a socially acceptable way of bullying other people. The bully challenges everything. All information is potentially false and at best biased. The bully has a mobile and expressive face. Most of the bullying actually takes place when the bully is listening. The expression on the face of the bully pours scorn, doubt, disbelief and even contempt on whatever is being said. This is rather difficult to counter because nothing has actually been said and you can hardly attack someone's facial expression:

'Your expression suggested that you did not like what I was saying. What was the matter?'

'Oh, nothing really.'

The bully is not in the least bit interested in the content of the conversation. The bully is only interested in the effect he or she has on others.

The attitude of the bully is that conversation is only another means of bullying.

Then there is the toady. The toady scurries to agree with the most powerful, the most important or the cleverest person in the discussion. In this way the toady seeks to get carried along as an ally, on the coat-tails of the other person. There might be something obviously sycophantic about the toady but this is not always apparent. It may just seem that one reasonable person is agreeing with another reasonable person. It is only when you have seen the toady change opinions from one group to another that you might suspect something.

'You are so very right.'

The toady does not like to answer questions because there is a risk the answer may not be approved by the powerful ally. The questions might be passed along: 'How would you answer that question?'

The attitude is that of a power game. If conversation is about power, why not have the most powerful ally?

Then there might be the innovator or ideas person. The innovator is bored by conventional opinions and arguments. The innovator awaits an opportunity to come up with a new, creative and unusual idea. This may be a new perception or way of looking at a problem. The new idea may be a suggested solution that goes beyond what has been suggested. The innovator is conscious that even if his or her new ideas are not directly acceptable, the ideas can serve as provocations to open up new lines of thought. The innovator does not really bother to follow the argument. Like a hawk, the innovator is waiting to pounce when there is a suitable opportunity. The innovator is a useful element in any discussion but the role can be overdone. If new ideas are suggested at every moment simply in order to be different, the conversation can turn into a fancy dress parade.

The attitude of the innovator is that only new ideas are fun and argument is boring.

Then there is the person who has seen and heard it all. There is an affected tiredness and boredom. Any line of argument is treated as 'old hat'. New ideas are treated as 'the same old ideas'. Such a person contributes very little and is a drain on any conversation. There is a 'negative enthusiasm', which absorbs and kills any real enthusiasm. This person implies that it is the duty of everyone else to amuse him or her with some new ideas.

The attitude is that of affected boredom.

THE BATTLE ATTITUDE

This attitude sees any conversation as a battle between two parties each of which has a point of view. The important thing is to win the battle. Exploration of the subject or the development of new ideas is not important at all.

In love and war all is fair and so it is with the battle attitude. Information is withheld if it would support the other point of view. (See also pages 14, 56, 89 and 104.)

This attitude is very close to that of lawyers in a court of law. It is a win-lose attitude. There is only going to be one winner. If appeasement seems to be offered it is only a ruse to lead on and trap the other side.

There is no mercy. The defeated side must clearly accept defeat.

THE EGO POWER GAME

Here the discussion is seen as an arena in which to exercise ego power. The discussion or conversation is there to be dominated.

This domination is not achieved in the 'battle mode'. On the contrary, there might be quite a lot of agreement in order to get allies on to your side. So long as you emerge as the dominant character, you do not have to win the argument.

There may be changes of strategy and changes of tactics according to how things develop. Dominance is a different concept from 'winning'.

In an election, the person playing the power game might be a 'populist' and get the most votes.

THE LEARNER ATTITUDE

Here the person enters the discussion with the clear intention of learning something. It is not a matter of proving you are right or convincing others of your point of view. The intention is to learn. There may be new ideas. There may be new insights and revelations. There may be new information. There may be new lines of thought. If at the end you can walk away having learned something new, then you have not wasted your time.

THE EXPLORER ATTITUDE

This is the same attitude as that of an explorer reaching new shores. There is a subject to be explored. How can some interesting minds explore that subject co-operatively? There will be different points of view just as different explorers may land at different points around an island. Can these different points of view be put together to give a more complete picture?

The explorer does not have to accept everything and can challenge information and ideas. But in doing so the explorer is interested in the truth, not in scoring debating points. The intention of the explorer is to lay out a full and complete picture. Everyone else is seen as an ally in achieving that aim.

THE CONSTRUCTIVE ATTITUDE

This is similar to the explorer but with one big difference. The explorer attitude seeks to examine the subject and lay it out clearly. The constructive attitude seeks to 'do something'. The constructive attitude seeks to 'design a way forward'. For the constructive attitude it is not enough just to 'know' something. There is a need also to 'do' something.

There is the famous quote of René Descartes: 'I think, therefore I am.'

Then there is a quote of my own: 'I do, therefore I matter.'

Reflection is not enough. Being aware is important but also not enough. There is a need to be constructive and to design a way forward.

THE FUN ATTITUDE

Conversation and discussion are an enjoyable use of the mind, just as sport is an enjoyable use of the body. So the main purpose of a conversation or discussion is to enjoy it and to help others enjoy it. (See also page 168.) There may be times when this is not enough and serious decisions have to be taken. On the whole, however, a conversation or discussion is an end in itself, just like a stroll through the woods might be an end in itself. Walking might keep you physically fit. In the same way, discussion can keep you mentally fit.

THE 'WHO CARES?' ATTITUDE

If you are going to be with other people you cannot just stand and stare at each other. Social behaviour requires that you talk to each other. This is like breathing. It just happens. We do not have to think consciously about breathing and we should not have to think about talking. Whatever chit-chat comes to mind will provide adequate communication. You can talk about last week's party or some latest gossip. It is the interaction with other people that matters – not what is said.

This is rather like saying people have to eat anyway so it does not matter what is cooked.

If you do enjoy interacting with other people, then you can double that pleasure by also enjoying what is said. Otherwise you might as well grunt at each other. You bother to make your appearance attractive, why not bother to make your conversation attractive?

ATTITUDE **SUMMARY**

1 Attitude is very much related to self-image.

2 There is the 'clever' person who has to be right and more clever than anyone else.

3 There is the 'guardian of values' who insists that only values matter and that he or she knows the right values.

4 There is the person who plays dumb and invites sympathy and help.

5 There are those who are so reasonable they never reach a conclusion or an opinion.

6 The bully uses conversation as only another means of bullying.

7 The toady allies himself or herself to the most powerful person in the group.

8 The innovator is only looking for opportunities to suggest creative new ideas.

9 The bored person affects to be bored and to have heard it all before.

10 There is the battle attitude of win-lose. There is the ego power game where domination is the intention.

11 The learner attitude always seeks to learn something new.

12 The explorer attitude seeks the truth and to fully understand the matter.

13 The constructive attitude seeks to design a way forward.

14 The fun attitude sees conversation as entertainment.

15 The 'who cares?' attitude believes that it does not matter at all what is said in a conversation or discussion.

18 🌴 starting
and topics

How do you start a conversation? What do you talk about?

There is the usual social chit-chat:

How is the new baby?
Did you enjoy your holiday in Mexico?
What is it like at college?
I am sorry to hear your aunt died.

Those sort of interchanges serve a very useful social function and are as important as any other type of conversation. But when the greetings have been made and the news and gossip exchanged, what then?

You can talk about the people in the room. You can talk about the room itself or the view from the window. What then?

CURRENT TOPICS

In a small town there may be a local scandal or some upcoming change. A local factory may be closing its doors or there may be an election. There might be some juicy gossip or a serious crime.

In larger communities, it is unlikely that the same issue would be on everyone's mind, so there is a need to find some current topic.

A major source of topics is the news. The news might have been delivered by radio, television or in the newspaper. A quick scan through the paper of the day should provide several possible topics. If the other person has read about something then this can be discussed right away. If the other person has not read about the topic then you have to explain it. There is validity in such an explanation because it is a current topic even if the other person is not aware of it. You might begin by saying: 'In the paper today there was this story . . .' Or: 'Did you see the report on television about . . .'

ON-GOING TOPICS

The run-up to an election provides an easy on-going topic. So would events like the Olympic Games. There might be on-going stories about the crematorium that neglected to cremate the bodies brought to it. Middle East violence might be an on-going topic. A news item about HIV or cloning could make these on-going topics. Try opening a conversation in this way:

Did you read the latest news about . . .
What do you think about the developments in . . .
I was surprised to see that . . .

You might find that the other party knows more than you on the issue or less than you. In one case you ask questions and in the other case you bring the other party up to speed on the matter.

There is an assumption that everyone knows about a major on-going topic and that therefore there is interest in discussing it. This interest may only be to provide material for further discussions on the topic with other people.

WHAT DO YOU DO?

This is the classic approach and it is a good one. The other person tells you his or her job or area of work. You then ask intelligent questions and gradually get to explore the whole area. For example:

Is it true that . . .
I have never understood why . . .
What happens when . . .
What are the most difficult areas in . . .

Some people enjoy talking about their work but others find it intensely boring. In any case, you need to be ready for the question to be bounced back to you:

I sell used cars. What about you?
I teach in a junior school. Where do you work?
I am a rocket scientist. What are you?

You should be ready to talk with interest about your own area of work. You should have worked this out in advance and pin-pointed in your mind the areas that are likely to be of interest to other people:

What people do not realise about a disc jockey is . . .
It becomes very tricky when . . .
It is very hard when you spend your life trying to tell people
    what they think they already know.
Looking after patients is the easy part. The difficult part is . . .
In surgery you have to know exactly what you are doing
    because you cannot go back and try it again.

The ensuing conversation does not have to stay within the area of a particular occupation. That might just be the starting point. A conversation that starts out looking at the advertising profession may move on to the ethics of persuasion. Would persuasion be morally and legally permissible if it were really effective?

In order to avoid a totally one-sided conversation, the person on the empty side seeks to pick out points for a discussion in which he or she can contribute.

FALSE STARTS

What do you do when the conversation is floundering? Neither party has much to say or seems interested in the subject. Do you struggle on and hope that interest will grow or do you abandon the subject as soon as possible?

In general, it is probably best to get out of a flagging subject. The hope of stimulating interest is not very realistic.

If you can pull a new line of conversation out of the existing discussion, that is probably best because it does not admit failure. You are having a discussion on increased airport security. You mention the new ultra-sound scanning system that can see through clothes. That leads you on to the research in Sweden that suggests that multiple ultra-sound scans of pregnant women might cause minimal brain damage to the unborn child. One claimed indicator of this minimal damage is the much higher than normal ratio of left-handed children. This in turn leads on to consideration of why left-handedness should suggest brain damage. Does this apply to all left-handedness? Several US presidents have been left-handed . . .

At other times there seems no way of moving forward:

This is getting nowhere. Let's talk about the mating habits of the hippopotamus.

I am much more interested in talking about the cloned cat than in talking about the new mayor.

NEW LEADS

In serious conversations you need to stay on-track. People who continually seek to pull the conversations off-track can be irritating. You would rather they went away and amused themselves somewhere else.

Most conversations, however, are not serious and interest is more important than staying on-track. New directions and leads can occur at any moment. Do you want to follow them? Do you want to initiate a new direction? (See also Chapter 13.)

Sometimes the new direction is heading towards an area that you know something about or an area that really interests you (even if you know little about it). Sometimes the new direction just seems interesting in itself.

Imagine a conversation about pensions. Someone suggests that you should specify your intended date of death and your pension would be adjusted accordingly. This leads on to a consideration whether people do actually 'will' themselves to die. When one partner in a devoted couple passes away, the other partner dies soon afterwards. On the other hand there are people who fight on and refuse to die, even when they are very sick. Through yoga or some other method, would it be possible to train yourself to die? Do some cultures actually do this? When aboriginals in Australia 'point bones' at a person, for example, that person often dies. In the end, aboriginal witch doctors have very little to do with pensions.

SHAPING

This is a form of deliberate diversion. There is an area that you enjoy talking about. There is an area which seems to interest other people (or so experience suggests). You make a deliberate effort to steer the conversation in that direction.

Imagine you are talking about the high divorce rate. Someone mentions that research shows that women usually initiate divorce. Research also shows that the main reason women initiate divorce is 'when they cannot influence their husband enough'. If your husband does not do what you tell him – get a new one! This leads on to the position of women in society. In Japan the women seem to be in the background but they wield a lot of power: they control all finances and family spending. This leads on to the matriarchal Zulu society. And you wanted to talk about Zulus all the time. You shaped the conversation to end up with Zulus.

Similarly: 'We were talking about oranges. Oranges supply us with vitamin C. But oranges only grow in certain climates. Where do people in other climates get their vitamin C? Where do people in Africa, for example, get their vitamin C? Where do Zulus get their vitamin C? Now talking about Zulus, do you know that . . .'

In this way you have been guided back to the Zulu principle!

If a particular person is known to want to talk only about a certain subject, however, that can become boring.

If every conversation is guided back to this same subject, others may prefer to keep away.

Some people are very skilful at guiding a conversation into areas they prefer. They do it subtly and there is no harm in it.

ANGER AND EMOTION

There can be certain topics which arouse a lot of anger and emotion, in general or only in certain people. It may even be that the topic arouses this emotion in one particular person. In other words, there is a lot of 'red hat' about the subject (see page 93).

Should you persist with the topic or should you change the subject?

You may want to probe and explore and seek the reasons behind the strong emotions.

You may decide that the strong emotions preclude any enjoyable conversation.

You may even enjoy provoking such emotions.

The choice is yours. You may feel challenged to see what lies behind the emotions. If you are confident enough to do this in a gentle way, there may be some value in this, even to the other party. But if you are not confident of your ability to do this in a sensitive way, it is best to drop the topic and to move on to another subject. Provocation for the sake of provocation is neither beautiful nor kind.

BORED

If someone sits back with the attitude 'amuse me', then you can decline that command. Smile and move on. A person who deliberately wants to be bored should be allowed that privilege. There is no reason why you should agree to be used in the process.

STARTING AND TOPICS **SUMMARY**

1 Greetings, the exchange of personal news and social chit-chat in general have a very important role in themselves. When this has been done there is a need to move on with a conversation.

2 There may be current local topics known to everyone in the community.

3 In larger communities the current topics may be taken from the news, for example, by scanning the newspaper.

4 There may be some on-going topics which everyone is likely to know about.

5 Asking what the other person 'does' is a safe standby opening. This topic need not dominate the entire conversation but can lead on to others.

6 If the conversation is getting nowhere, it is best to change subjects and to start again.

7 If the conversation does not have a serious purpose, be ready to open up and to follow new directions which lead to more interesting areas.

8 You can seek to 'shape' a conversation to reach an area you really want to talk about. Try not to do this often enough to bore everyone.

9 Where a topic seems to arouse strong anger or emotion, you may seek, sensitively, to explore the reasons behind this. Otherwise turn to another topic.

10 If a person decides to be bored, you have no obligation to offer that sort of service. Smile and move on.

11 Developing areas of interest to you and knowing how to talk about such areas is another attribute of the beautiful mind.

12 A really skilled conversationalist can create interest from any topic whatsoever.

❦ conclusion

A beautiful body and a beautiful face age and grow old. A beautiful mind does not age and, in fact, can become ever more beautiful.

A beautiful body and a beautiful face without a beautiful mind can be boring. A beautiful mind without a beautiful body or a beautiful face can still be attractive.

This book has been about how to develop a beautiful mind. This means a mind that is attractive to others as well as to yourself. It is not just a matter of sitting in a corner and having beautiful thoughts. It is a beautiful mind in action. The action is not that of solving a complex problem but the action of exploring a subject in discussion and conversation. It is in this context that others can see how beautiful your mind can be.

Although conversation is the theme that runs through the book, the habits and skills of thinking learned in that context can be applied whenever you have to use your mind.

This book is not a novel which you read through rapidly to see how it all works out. You can return again and again to different sections. If you take someone who has never seen a game of tennis to watch a tennis match, that person may after a while consider that he or she 'understands' the game of tennis. But understanding the game of tennis is not the same as playing the game of tennis. So you need to practise and observe the habits mentioned in the book. Watch yourself in action. Watch others in action and relate what you see to what you read in the book. In this way you build up your skill. In this way you develop a beautiful mind.

You may agree with what I have written. You may disagree with what I have written. You may seek to modify what I have written out of your own experience or to fit your own personality. You may wish to amplify certain points. You may use the points I have made to stimulate further thinking in your own mind. You may choose to ignore some, or all, of what I have written. It must always be your choice.

ENJOYMENT

Sport is enjoyable. Why should the use of your mind not be as enjoyable as the use of your body? The use of your mind in conversation and discussion should be enjoyable – it should be a form of entertainment. As you practise using your mind, you enjoy that use and at the same time build up your thinking skill towards an even more beautiful mind. You can enjoy agreeing and disagreeing. You can enjoy being different and applying different values. You can enjoy asking questions and learning when to interrupt and when not to interrupt.

Imagine you are playing tennis and at the same time can watch a video of yourself playing tennis. It is like that with the skills outlined in this book. You can enjoy using them and you can, at the same time, watch yourself using them.

SKILL

Our natural habits of thinking and conversation, with the emphasis on the 'battle' of argument and seeking to prove people wrong, are not at all beautiful. War is never beautiful. An ego seeking to dominate is not beautiful at all.

The most important thing to remember is that everything put forward in this book is part of the 'skill' of thinking. You do not need a high IQ. You do not need to be well educated. You do not need to be full of information. Anyone can develop a beautiful mind if he or she sets out to do so.

❦ the **conversation** club

The Conversation Club is a group of people who agree to meet on a regular basis to practise and enjoy the art of conversation.

There is a dual emphasis. One is on improving those skills which give a beautiful mind. The other emphasis is on enjoyment of the use of the mind in conversation.

The members of the Club may be all from one family, or from other families, neighbours, work colleagues, friends – or even brought together by notices in the library or other places. The only qualifications are that a member should speak and understand the language that is going to be used (there is no need to be excellent in the language), and motivation. Motivation is the key qualification. If all the members are motivated then the Club will be successful.

NUMBERS

Ideally, a club should consist of six people, but any number from one to six is possible. How do you have a conversation if there is only one person? You need a tape recorder and then you speak into it, acting out both sides of a conversation. Then you play the recording back and observe what has been happening.

There can be more than six people but this would mean that many members would then be in the position of 'audience' and would observe rather than contribute. If this is the case then there is no limit on the number of those present.

In general, if there are a lot of people, it would be better to split up into separate groups each of which runs its own session.

REGULARITY

It is very important that the meetings take place regularly, at the same time and, preferably, at the same place. The regularity and ritual is important in order to keep things going.

The frequency of meetings could be once a week, once a fortnight or once a month, depending on the wishes of the members. The meetings could, for example, be held every Tuesday evening from six to eight o'clock. The meetings could be held on the first Thursday in every month. It is much harder to remember fortnightly meetings.

Meetings should last from two to three hours. There can be shorter meetings if there are few people. Longer meetings would become tiring and even boring.

THE ORGANISER

This is the key person. This is the person who sets up the Club in the first place and who keeps it going. This is a person who is motivated, energetic and a good organiser. If there is a person with these qualities then that person remains the organiser. The role is not rotated. The chairing of particular sessions can rotate but the overall organisation need not. Things fall apart very quickly if there is poor organisation even for one session.

During the session itself, the organiser can act as organiser for that session as well. Competence is important. There needs to be strict discipline during the session otherwise the session can degenerate into a shapeless discussion. It is up to the organiser to hold things together. If the group wishes then the organiser role for a session can rotate. This can be risky, however, and is not recommended.

FORMAT

There is a tight format and structure to the session. In general, there are participants who take part in the conversation and then there are observers who observe and comment on what is said.

Those who wish to set up and register Conversation Clubs can obtain full details on format and structure at: www.edwarddebono.com/conversationclubs

AGENDA AND TOPICS

Registered clubs will receive a regular package of suggested topics and agendas. They do not have to use these and can, of course, create agendas of their own – provided they keep in mind certain important guidelines.

The advantage of an agenda that is given to you is that you are 'forced' to tackle difficult subjects that you may never have chosen otherwise. In this way members are challenged in their thinking.

ACHIEVEMENT

There are several levels of achievement:

1 *Holding and enjoying regular sessions of the Club and being able to invite guests.*
2 *Listening to the comments of the 'observers' and watching how conversation skills develop.*
3 *The use of a special scoring system for ideas, evidence and values.*

4 *It may be possible to publish on the Internet brief outcomes from those Clubs who submit the results of their sessions.*

Through these Clubs, thinking becomes a hobby and you get the sense of achievement that all hobbies provide.

It is important to note that the achievement is not the same as the achievement of a debating group where 'win' or 'lose' is the measure of achievement. In a Conversation Club everyone wins. If a group of people go swimming they can all swim. That is the achievement. You do not need to have a race to show achievement.

CROSS VISITS

Registered clubs will be put in touch with each other and may choose to visit each other for mixed sessions. Everyone will know the rules and will have had experience playing within the rules.

Ballet is created from thirteen basic steps. That is the framework within which you set out to be creative. That is the framework within which you are free.

Similarly, without conversation frameworks some sessions would be wonderful but many more would be a mess.

Youngsters can be invited to take part in the sessions so learning useful habits at a young age.

RANGE OF ACTIVITIES

The information package will lay out a range of possible activities during a session.

For example, there might be an exercise in which those taking part in the discussion pause and the others are asked to 'pick out the concepts' in what is being put forward.

On another occasion there might be a request to 'lay out the difference between the two points of view'.

In this way the skills mentioned in this book can be learned and developed.

There is much more to a conversation than just having something to say.

The registered Clubs will be known as: 'The Edward de Bono Conversation Clubs'. This is for the purpose of branding and to distinguish these Clubs from other organisations.

For the same reason lapel badges will be made available for those who may want to indicate to others they meet that they belong to a Conversation Club and therefore abide by the rules.

For further information about the Conversation Clubs see www.edwarddebono.com or www.edwdebono.com.